COMMUNISM AND SOCIALISM

C. F. W. WALTHER

Western Front BOOKS

ISBNs:

978-1-959666-28-8 (paperback)

978-1-959666-27-1 (ebook)

Originally published with a subtitle: *A Stenographic Report Of Four Lectures Delivered, And By Resolution Of The Congregation, First Published*, from the *Minutes of The First German Evangelical Lutheran Congregation*, U. A. C. at Saint Louis, Missouri by C. F. W. Walther, D. D. and Translated from the German by Rev. D. Simon and published in 1879 by *Concordia Publishing House*, St. Louis Missouri.

Subsequent 1947 revised English translation published by *The Lutheran Research Society*.

Translated from German by Rev. D. Simon, M. A..

Lightly revised, corrected, and annotated by Joseph Dindinger for Wise Path Books in 2023.

Contents

Translator's Preface to the 1879 Edition

That our American people may be enabled the better to understand the true character of Communism, that they may see its blackness in the light of God's Word, that they may be warned against its dreadful influences, that man may be benefited, and God glorified, this English translation of Dr. Walther's excellent lectures is herewith dedicated to the American Public, but especially to those who may desire to acquaint themselves with the secret of our nation's troubles.

The translator has endeavored to give Dr. Walther's ideas in smooth English, without confining himself throughout to the original wording. Rev. C. T. Steck of Homer, Pa., assisted the undersigned in carefully criticizing the language used, in consequence of which he hopes the work will need no further criticism after leaving the press.

God's blessing accompany this little work then and cause it to do its work right nobly.

D. SIMON, M. A.
    Translator.

Publisher's Preface to the 1879 Edition

The undersigned yielded with reluctance to the earnest request of the Lutheran Congregation of this place to publish a stenographic report of extemporaneous lectures on Socialism and Communism, called forth by special circumstances, delivered at four evening sessions of the congregation. The publisher hopes, however, that the indulgent and unprejudiced reader will overlook the formal defects which were unavoidable in the circumstances under which these lectures originated, and he also hopes that the reader will not inconsiderately reject the truth presented in these pages because of these defects. May that which is here presented, occasioned as it was by the special circumstances of the congregation of this place, serve to call attention, also in other circles, to a question that is becoming more and more a burning one, even among Christians, and may it also give them occasion to answer from Scripture, reason and history, every form of this question, in which it may be presented, and that more thoroughly than time would allow.

THE PUBLISHER.

M. C. Barthel, Agt.

Publisher's Foreword To The 1947 Edition

These lectures by Dr. C. F. W. Walther, first President of the Missouri Synod, have been practically unread for over half a century. Although given almost seventy-five years ago to a local group in St. Louis, they are as up-to-date as if written to apply in 1947.

Walther is almost prophetic when he writes so many years ago, at the time the labor movement was in its infancy: "The ignorant are to be drummed together and organized into labor-unions, that in these unions the seed of socialism and communism may be sown, and when the seed has come to maturity, there will be enough muscle to accomplish the desired end by force ... but it must be remembered that these unions are only instruments in the hands of socialists and communists, in fact, a school of the socialists."

While every phase of our national and personal life has been invaded by the virus of communism, the truth stands today that the labor unions of our land are the most affected. The communists are in the government, in the church, in the schools, in politics, in the theater, etc., but nowhere are they as firmly entrenched as in the labor unions. They possibly represent only 2% of the membership in the CIO, for example. Yet these few have gained a stranglehold on the many, which is making it very difficult to break at this late date. For seventy-five years, the Marxists have been working in America. The sleepy population is beginning slowly to arouse. Is it too late? Is the populace aware that the Marxists are not being converted merely because communism has become unpopular? They have the same evil heart, the same evil designs on America. They must be watched, for they are going into different places to hide behind new fronts. This history of communism will greatly benefit Christians who want the truth about its background, aims, and plots. Walther has done a great service to this generation.

In his day, several hundred people heard or read these tremendous lectures. Now thousands have the opportunity to profit from them. During the most recent years of our history in America, we have seen individual freedom waning. Not all see the handwriting on the wall. By God's grace, the day of freedom for mankind may still come. There is weighty evidence to believe that if Dr. Walther had spoken in 1940 as he wrote in these lectures, he might have been indicted and involved in the unjust mass sedition trial held in Washington under the New Deal regime at its worst. Thus far, the liberty to write and speak the truth has gone from America.

May these lectures awaken in the leaders of the Church a desire to be even more fully acquainted with the tools of satan so that they may be all the more prepared to lead the sheep and fight the good fight of faith. Our beloved Church will need this great awakening if we are to celebrate the close of the second century in the same grace and spirit we have completed the first. God grant it for Jesus' sake!

The text of Rev. Simon's English translation has been left almost intact. Little has been omitted, and little changed. The changes were intended to fit more into the usage of our time, but enough of the old has been left to remind us that this is truly a voice speaking to us from the past.

———

This collection is republished by The Lutheran Research Society in commemoration of the Centennial of the Missouri Synod Lutheran Church of which Dr. C. F. W. Walther was the first president.

———

THE PUBLISHER
THE LUTHERAN RESEARCH SOCIETY
Lawrence Reilly, A. B., B. D., Director.
September 1947

First Lecture

O God, Thou has created man, originally
good and happy, and placed him in a
beautiful Paradise, that this might be his
home. But alas! man has fallen from
Thee, and because of this fall, has become
a poor, wretched creature, and his life on
earth has become a life of toil and
trouble.

But instead of accusing himself and pleading
for Thy mercy, man accuses Thee, denies
the providence and government of Thy
mercy, and flees from Thee in despair, or
gives expression, in his heart, to the
fearful words: "There is no God!"

In mercy keep us from such great blindness
and sin, and enlighten our understand-
ing, that, midst the troubles of earth, we
may with deep humility, acknowledge
the result of our apostasy, and govern

*Thou our hearts that we may not contend
with Thee our merciful Creator, but
humble ourselves, in the midst of our toil
and trouble, under Thy almighty hand,
patiently await Thy help, and comfort
ourselves with the fact, that the sufferings
of this present time are not worthy to be
compared with the glory that shall be
revealed in Thy children in the world to
come.*

*Have mercy on the entire human race in
their affliction, draw them by Thy Word
to Thee, help them out of every bodily
and spiritual trouble, and open to them
at last the eternal kingdom of Thy joy
and glory. Yea, do this for the sake of
Jesus Christ, the common Savior of the
world. Amen.*

———

As is known to the congregation, the occasion of this meeting is twofold. The first is the appearance of a daily paper here in St. Louis, which would pretend to be the organ of the laborers, in consequence of which, many, particularly younger members of our congregation, have also made it their paper. The second occasion is the formation of the so-called Labor-Unions, which are to represent the interests of the laborers over against the employers.

If that paper were in reality the organ of the laborers,

which would represent the interests of the laboring class in a legitimate manner, who could find fault if any laborer would select it as his paper and would even prefer it above other secular papers? And if the Labor-Unions were no more than were the Fraternities, Guilds, Tradesmen's-Unions, and Clubs of Germany, who could make it a matter of conscience to join one of them? Does not even the Apostle Paul expressly declare that if Christians would no longer unite themselves with the children of the world, no not even in civil and business affairs, they would be necessitated to leave the world? But alas! the state of affairs is entirely different here. The said paper is not, for example, by any means an organ intended for the laborers alone, but it has for its aim the propagation of the modern communistic ideas, peaceably if possible, or forcibly, and that by possible fire and sword, if necessary. It is only too well known that the Labor-Unions have been conceived and called into existence by the Communists and Socialists, and are intended by them to be nothing else than schools of communism and socialism.

That no one might think these declarations unfounded, I have secured several copies of this paper, called "Volksstimme des Westens" (The voice of the people of the West), without, however, inquiring which number might give the best idea of its character. I have nevertheless secured copies which show its character plainly. In the number dated Dec. 24, 1877, there is a continuation of a novel, written by the editor of the paper, Dr. A. Otto-Walster, in which we read, among other things, the following:

"It shall be our chief concern to show that man, with his claims on material prosperity, need not be directed to another world, that he can and should find such prosperity here on earth, and would in this connection call attention to the verses in Heine's, 'Wintermaerchen':

> "A song that's new and truthful too,
> Dear friends, I will indite for you—
> A song of heaven here on earth,
> Claimed by right of human birth.
>
> We would be happy here below
> Nor longer suffer want and woe!
> The lazy belly shall not spoil
> What faithful hands have won by toil.
>
> On earth there grows enough of bread;
> For all mankind the table's spread;
> Where rose and myrtle spring to please,
> Why see, there too grow sugar peas.
>
> Aye, sugar peas for best and worst,
> As soon the pregnant pods may burst;
> Celestial joys we leave indeed
> To angels and the sparrow breed."[1]

It seems to me that one single quotation of this character should suffice to cause us to wonder how a Christian, who accepts the Holy Scriptures as God's Word, believes in Christ, and has the hope of eternal life, could support such a paper. Everyone can see that this is an atheistic paper, whose editor believes neither in God nor eternal life, but ridicules both. Should he even say that he believes in God and also in a future life, it matters not. We look at what he publishes in his paper. He must suffer himself to be judged by that, and his paper takes the position of atheistic communism!

But observe another proof that this paper is of a communistic character. Had I taken the pains to examine the whole volume, I could no doubt have produced many more proofs, but these few will serve our purpose well. This is what is said in the number dated Dec. 15:

"Fire, water, air, and earth are the four so-called elements of nature, of which Divinity gave one man as much as the other. Who will, who can deny it? You, there-fore, see, worthy Dr. (it is an article against a certain Dr. Holland) that this communism, recommended by our 'Lord Jesus Christ' to his pupils and followers, has been in existence since the creation of the world and of man."

Our beloved Lord Jesus Christ is accordingly to be considered the chief-communist! It is further said:

"An all-wise and beneficent God is himself the author, and 'Christ' the Son, only carries into execution what God, the 'Father' had planned and determined from the beginning."

It is worthy of note that the terms Christ, and God, the Father, are given in quotations. By this, the writer would give his opponent to understand: "I am now speaking with your understanding; of course I don't believe in a Christ, neither do I believe in a God, the Father. But I am going to fight for once with your own weapons. You profess to yield submission to the written Word, as you term it. Very well, I will convict you from your own Word of God, and show you that if you would be a faithful adherent to the Bible, you must also become a communist." This is what he means to say. —He continues:

"This is God's command and Christ's doctrine." Again: "The laboring men of America do not intend to cast themselves under the wheels of a so-called civilization, which is nothing but barbarism, to be crushed to death, and to see their children condemned to eternal poverty and eternal misery, so that a few fortunate ones may continue in their idleness and wealth. They will no longer kiss the hand that strikes the blow. They will cease to hug the chains with which they are fettered. They will rise up, they are rising up already, in the glory of their power and manhood, to crush to atoms this foul and hideous monster, to assert their liberty like men, and thus to become free and happy."

This is yet moderate language. But everyone acquainted with history knows where this is leading. It is the lightning in the distance which precedes that most dreadful thunderstorm, which these men would call down upon this generation. If they cannot gain their ends in peace, they will resort to violence and bloodshed. This giant, by whom they fancy themselves to be trodden under foot, they would crush to atoms.

As pertains to the working-men's party, of which every labor-union is a part, we find their program in the number for Nov. 30. In this program, we read in the very beginning:

"As civil liberty, without economical independence, is a mere form of speech, the party begins its struggles within the sphere of economy, and demands that all material for labor become the property of the society, so that instead of paying wages, the income of the society, as the joint fruits of labor, may be justly divided among the members."

When the communists say that material shall become the property of the society, they would not limit it to their circle. For, if a number of men would realize this idea only among themselves, so far as possible, we might calmly look on. Everyone has the right to deny himself certain privileges; and, by way of agreement, unite with others. There have been different societies of this character. They, however, refer to society in general, to the whole human race; that is where they would realize these ideas. They would overthrow the existing social relations and arrange them according to their principles. The following are some of their principles:

"No one shall own any real estate, but this shall be common property, and shall be managed only by certain persons," although the various propositions pertaining to this matter differ widely, as we shall presently see. It is then further said: "machinery, ways of transfer, etc. " It is left to the reader to supply anything he pleases under the "etc." This embraces a great deal. The brethren who enter these labor-unions little anticipate what is implied in this "etc." Neither do they anticipate what is implied in the idea, that no one shall own any real estate. They do not consider, either, what fearful overthrow of the order of things it would involve to realize this. They also demand: "The introduction of the eight-hour law and the punishment of all who transgress it." Let every Christian reader decide for himself whether a Christian can enter into such a labor-union. I am of the opinion that he cannot, without violating his conscience. He cannot become a member of an association, which has in view the overthrow of the world, either peaceably if possible, or forcibly if necessary.

It is of importance, however, what Mr. Walster himself discloses in his paper, dated Nov. 30, 1877, concerning the condition of the labor-unions in America. He was assailed by the editor of a Milwaukee paper, the "Milwaukee Social-ist." He shall, says the Milwaukee editor, confine himself to the field of politics, for here alone can the laboring-man finally gain his liberty. Only get the government into your hands once, and you can readily change all the present rela-tions. The establishment of labor-unions can only detain a good cause. Before a change could be effected in this way, the laboring-men would die of starvation.

To this, Mr. Walster answers:

"We do certainly not belong to those, who, in their one-sided agitation, would solve the social question by means of corporations (labor-unions), and yet we must unreservedly acknowledge the value of these corporations, in that by their means the socialistic propaganda (principles) are agitated and made known."

He means to say that he does not expect much to be accomplished by means of these labor-unions in the near future; he knows how weak they are, even when in the most prosperous condition. But it must be remembered that these unions are only instruments in the hands of socialists and communists, in fact, a school of the socialists. The ignorant are to be drummed together and organized into labor-unions, that in these unions the seed of socialism and communism may be sown, and when the seed has come to maturity, there will be enough muscle to accomplish the desired end by force, if the desired end cannot be attained peaceably. For it is even true that there is a greater number of poor people, who must support themselves by manual labor, than of those who live from their capital, be it from the interest of the capital or from speculations made with the capital in certain enterprises into which they may have entered; and if the masses were once won over to the socialistic ideas, the communists would undoubtedly gain the day. Verily they could turn the world upside down, and drown all their opponents in their own blood. The idea is certainly not a stupid one. But whether it will be realized is another question. —He says further:

"There is, for example, here in St. Louis, one section of the cabinet-makers-union. It is composed of socialists and non-socialists. The socialists developed their propaganda in this section and succeeded in gaining a large majority for socialism; the consequence is that in this section, the socialistic question is discussed at every meeting, whereby statistics are brought out and systematized greatly to the encouragement of our agitation."

Mr. Walster would accordingly say: "Behold, I am doing this more shrewdly than you. You would obtain support for our communism and socialism only by means of political agitations. Do it then, but if you do no more, you are a fool. Our method will accomplish more. We gather those together who are not socialists and convert them into socialists." He means to say that the labor-unions are but schools of socialism and communism. And now I ask: What Christian would enter into such a labor-union and become the willing servant of such a revolution? No Christian can do so with a clear conscience; it is alone the place for him who denies the existence of a God.

Another testimony that the labor-unions are nothing else than the institutions of the communists, used for the accomplishment of their ends, is the following: The English communists cast lots for the benefit of the prisoners of New Caledonia, but not for the benefit of all the prisoners, but only for those who were transported there from France, because in the year 1871, they had committed those well-known, fearful communistic outrages. When the Prussians concluded peace at Paris, the entire French national guard was permitted to retain its firearms. This was done on the part of Germany because it was considered good policy, inasmuch as it was feared that a revolution would break out since all kinds of people had gathered together in Paris. They had miscalculated. Nearly all these firearms got into the hands of the communists who made use of the power thus acquired in a frightful slaughter. They established a so-called Commune, and took possession of the city. At once they shot several of the generals, who had remained faithful to the government, shot the arch-bishop and other prelates and priests, erected barricades, and from thence shot into the crowd standing on the opposite side; and declared that if they would not gain the victory, they would level Paris with the ground. "War against the palaces" was their watch-word. This was faithfully carried out. In March, the fearful catastrophe began, and in May, it ended. Blood had flown in streams, and the most magnificent buildings lay in ashes. Woe to that city if the Communists had gained the victory! And for those, who at that time committed those fearful outrages, there are now lots cast. Pertaining to this matter, and in its defense, our labor unions and their branches are addressed in the following language;

"Laboring-men! The revolution of the 18th of March has been shamefully misrepresented by the Capitalists of both hemispheres. You are interested in this revolution: for the principles for which they fought, you have adopted into your platforms. Every one of you is responsible for them, and to deny them would be nothing less than betrayal. You are most intimately united with those who are suffering for the crime of losing the victory in the struggle for rights which we ourselves demand."

This is, however, a declaration that the labor unions of our land are in reality only branches of that labor union which has its center in England. This society was founded in 1869 by a Jew named Karl Marx, at which time the directors of the association made the following declarations: "This association declares itself for Atheism." That is, it declares there is no God, for an Atheist is one who denies the existence of a God. "It demands the abolition of all religion, the substitution of science for faith, human righteousness for the righteousness of God. the abrogation and suppression of marriage . . . We demand that the people make the laws directly for the people, that all laws of inheritance be abolished, and that all real estate become common property."

These are the principles on which the international labor union is founded. It is called international because the members are to be gathered, not only from one nation, but from every nation on earth.

I now ask again whether a Christian can connect himself with an association, of which he knows that it would carry out the principles just mentioned? It matters not whether the laboring-man who enters into the association would carry them out or not—he belongs to the association which holds to this purpose. In Paris, it was evident that many indeed had belonged to this association, who were merely interested in the society and little thought of being involved in a revolution; but when the fearful moment had come and all were drunk with excitement, there was no escape: whoever belonged to this society had to expect a bullet through his head or cooperate with them. And those who have been in these associations for many years have not the Christian courage to say: "No, if such are your intentions, I can no longer go with you." A great number have been drawn into the society, deny God and their Savior, and are on the way that leads to a fearful end, both in time and eternity.

So much to show the character of that paper and the socialistic labor unions. But the question is of an altogether different character: What shall we say of Communism? i.e., the system according to which all goods shall be equally divided; or, What shall we say of Socialism? i.e., the system according to which no person shall own any property, but by united labor, all becomes the property of the society? The former are more radical, the latter less, but as a matter of fact, the most radical are always victorious. This was the case in France. Those who began the agitation had not intended to do what was afterward done, but those much more radical than they overpowered them brought them to the guillotine, until finally the most radical became leaders and ruled, until God brought it to an end. I have a few points noted down, which we will now consider, if the congregation will indulge me. This is the question:

WHY SHOULD AND CAN NO REASONABLE MAN, MUCH LESS A CHRISTIAN, TAKE PART IN

THE EFFORTS OF COMMUNISTS AND SOCIALISTS?

I. Because these efforts are contrary to reason, nature, and experience for

1. it is a fact that men are not equal;
2. it is a fact that men are naturally selfish;
3. it is a fact that happiness does not consist in external advantages:
4. it is a fact well established by experience that the communists have never attained their professed end, and only introduced sorrow and suffering.

II. Because these efforts are contrary to Christianity, for

1. What is adduced from the Scriptures in their favor, either proves nothing, or proves the contrary. It is urged: *(a) that according to the Holy Scriptures, God gave man the earth and all things in the earth for his possession;* (b) *that the first congregation at Jerusalem had a certain community of goods; (c) that Christ did not only warn against striving after riches, but also commanded: "Sell that thou hast, and distribute unto the poor, and thou shall have treasure in heaven: and come, follow me." Luke 18:22.; (d) that according to the teachings of Christ, the*

laborers in the vineyard should receive equal wages.

2. The efforts of the socialists and communists are in conflict with definite doctrines of Christianity, to wit: *(a) the doctrines of personal property, as involved in the seventh commandment, "Thou shall not steal," and taught elsewhere in Scripture;* (b) *the doctrine taught in the fifth commandment and in other passages, that the government alone has the power of the sword;* (c) *the doctrine of the sanctity of marriage, as set forth in the sixth commandment and elsewhere:* (d) *the difference recognized in the Bible not only (1)* between parents and children, man and wife, master and servant, employer and employed, but also (2) between rich and poor; (e) *the scriptural doctrine that God would use men's adversities for their spiritual welfare;* (f) *the scriptural doctrine that man shall eat his bread in the sweat of his face; (g) the scriptural doctrine that human happiness is not to be sought in this world, but in God and in the hope of a recompense and equalization[2] in the world to come, and in the hope of eternal life; and finally* (h) *the scriptural doctrine that the source of all misery in this world is sin.*

III. BECAUSE THE CHARGES OF COMMUNISM AGAINST THE CHURCH AND THE CHRISTIAN RELIGION, THAT THESE RATHER HINDER THAN PROMOTE THE MATERIAL WELFARE OF MAN, ARE UNFOUNDED AND UNJUST, TO WIT:

1. the charge that the Church is in league with wealth, oppression, and tyranny, and
2. the charge that the Church is incapable of relieving human suffering.

These are the points to be considered if we, as Christians, wish to define our position in regard to communism and socialism.

————

We are opposed to the efforts of the socialists:

I. BECAUSE THESE EFFORTS ARE CONTRARY TO REASON, NATURE, AND EXPERIENCE.

It is madness to think of accomplishing anything contrary to reason, nature, and experience. The heathen of old have already declared: "And if you would drive nature out of man with a pitchfork, you will not accomplish it."[3] Nature cannot be driven out; she has, to a certain extent, become identic with us, i.e., we ourselves are our embodied nature.

The first thing we have to consider is:

1. It is a fact that men are not equal.

There are no two things on earth absolutely identical. Of course, these communists do not believe in the existence of God; but by this, they have not yet put Him out of the way. This great, almighty, omniscient God has shown that He creates nothing a second time. He has created no two things alike. There are no two leaves exactly alike; yea, not an atom can be found that would be exactly like another atom. Throughout the creation, everything differs from everything else. God is accordingly not an equalizer, but one who creates dissimilar things. Man cannot, to save his life, make two things equal. The principle that all things shall be made alike is not founded in nature. The same is evident in man. One man is a deep thinker but has no wealth of ideas nor a prolific ingenuity; another is healthy and strong, another is an invalid; one man is particularly gifted for mental labor, another for mechanical labor; one has an inclination to this, another to something altogether different; one is naturally economical, another naturally extravagant; one is disposed to anger, another to calmness under all circumstances; one becomes angry only when put to the severest test, another burns with rage at the slightest provocation. These are only a few instances, but now consider what we ourselves have experienced with regard to the diversities of men. And to these instances can be added a great number in which the relations are of a most diversified character. It would therefore be altogether unnatural to place human society in such a condition that all would be equal.

The communists will not deny that if they would insti-tute a communistic State, in whatever manner they might undertake to do it, they must so arrange matters that the society of man becomes an organized body. But in this, there must be rulers and subjects. Therefore just as soon as they would realize their ideas, they must also begin with the extreme opposite, appoint rulers and declare to the others: "You must suffer yourselves to be governed by these."

But the communists will perhaps object to this and say that we misunderstand them. "We would not have all men equal," they say, "we only want equality in possessions, enjoyments, and the like. Otherwise, we would leave man as he is."

This objection is worthless. Equality in these things presupposes mental equality. For just as soon as there is no mental equality, the communists cannot establish an equality in possessions, much less in happiness. They would have equality in possessions that all may be equally happy; but in a humanity so diversified, happiness is produced in altogether different ways. One is made happy by this means, another by that. Many a one thinks: "it would be dreadful to be in this or that man's place;" and another one thinks: "I would not be in your position," I, for example, am happy to think that I am a theologian, another one thinks, it would be a dog-life to sit at these books from morning till evening, day after day. He would not spend his time in idle-ness, but this kind of work is not to his taste. There are indeed communists who say that when they shall have established such an order, they will ask each one with regard to his inclinations and talents. We would then say: "You shall do the tailoring for us all, you shall make the shoes, you shall carry on commerce, and the like." But the very thought of realizing such ideas is ludicrous. Who would then say: "I will clean out the sewers!" Who would say: "I am especially inclined to this work!" No one would likely be found for such work.

Again: here is a large hospital in a communistic state. For alas! the communists cannot make men equal in health. This they should be able to accomplish first of all, for it is an essential part of universal happiness that one man have just as good health as another. Then imagine: Here is a hospital in which there are sick, suffering from the most loathsome diseases. Day and night, there is a fearful stench. A single hour in this atmosphere may cause disease. The communistic ruler would then say: "Who is inclined to go to this place and take care of the sick?"' The stillness of death would be the answer. Everyone would say: "Why should it be in my place to go? There must be equality!"—and because of equality, no one does anything. Is this not extreme folly? The paradise to be realized by having all things equal looks very well on paper. This, then, the socialist, believes; but only so long as they do not take into consideration the relations which would be called into existence by carrying out their principles. Their ideas are mere phantoms.

Communism paints a picture of a fool's paradise and thinks that if only all property becomes common property, then all will have equal claims upon it, and this will become a glorious world. But it is altogether overlooked that many things would be involved which would make this impossible. The communists would have all possessions equally divided. But if all have been made equal today by such division, how will it be tomorrow? One locks up his money in a drawer, another spends his for drink in a tavern, and still, another runs through his money at even worse places. By tomorrow the equality is again destroyed.

Infatuated communists! They well see that they are an unhappy people. They bitterly experience the wretchedness of the world and especially now in these perilous times. They experience this, but they do not consider the cause of all this. They have lost God, and with Him, the noblest good; this is why they have no comfort. And now the world is to be improved, and that by means of an equalization; for they think, "there is certainly enough wealth in the world that everyone might enjoy as much as his heart desires." But what folly! Even if everyone would agree to such arrangements, it is evident that they would soon become tired of being made equal with others. Therefore we say in the second place:

2. It is a fact that men are naturally selfish.

The communists must admit that men will indeed never peaceably suffer themselves to be reduced to equality; they must be forced to it. But it would be contrary to their own principles continually to force people to submit to these new arrangements. The paradise which they would establish would then be a perfect hell; the social relations would become worse than ever. Man is selfish by nature. One whose heart has not been changed thinks of self first. Such a person will say: " 'I' comes first, and then 'I' comes another time, and then my neighbor may have a bit of a chance." Man's heart is naturally full of envy, ambition, and avarice. These are all wild beasts which abide in the natural man, and which the communist will never be able to control with his new social arrangements. Men are not satisfied with just what they need and more than the necessities the socialists could never give. No, the majority of men want more; yes, they want a great deal, and the more they obtain, the greater becomes their desire for riches. If one has gained a small amount of wealth, he is like the man who drinks the water of the sea, which never quenches his thirst, but increases it and makes it more scorching.

It is a truth which no one can deny, dreadful as it is, that man is naturally selfish, and a selfish person will not be made equal with others unless those with whom he is to be made equal are by far his superiors. All those who are in favor of the new communist regulations for society are in favor of them because they expect to have their conditions improved. After considering your own experience with men, ask yourself whether you believe that many would be found who would consent to the new regulation of things if they knew that they would thereby reduce their present circumstances? No, with the exception of a few fanatics, only those would consent to such regulations who expected to improve their condition by doing so. This is the reason why the communists can attain their desired ends in no other way than by the shedding of blood, by murder, and arson.

Whenever they have aimed to accomplish anything practical, they have resorted to these means. The introducers of these ideas saw at once that there was no way of accomplishing their purpose except by striking off the heads of their opponents. However, this is evidently frenzy; for although they should strike off the heads of thousands, yes, of millions, new opponents to this system would continue to make their appearance. How much blood has been shed for this cause in France already during the first revolution in the last decade of the past century! Blood flowed in streams. The beginning was made with the king; he had to be beheaded, together with his wife and daughters. They next turned upon the bishops, the priests, the wealthy, and the most eminent ministers, who had formerly assisted in ruling the land. But what was accomplished? It matters not how much blood had been spilt; thousands and thousands of secret enemies were only waiting for their deliverance from this reign of terror. Is it not terrible that those who would make the entire world happy by the establishment of a paradise, must begin by shedding streams of blood? Everyone, not of their opinion, is put to death and frequently with the most terrible tortures!

It is absolutely true that men are naturally selfish, and this, too, shows the folly of attempting to help society by means of an external equalization. Help can be secured only by removing selfishness. Then it may be accomplished. But as long as man continues in his selfishness, it is the greatest folly imaginable to attempt to make all men equal in wealth, equal in honor. —In France, they even went so far as to say: "No one shall excel the other in education," and to symbolize the idea that nothing but equality should be recognized, all the tall, slender trees had to be cut down. It was already determined that the steeples should also be torn down. For doing this, they might seem to have had some reason, inasmuch as the steeples pointed to heaven, of which they want to know nothing, for they would have their heaven here on earth.

Should a man, for example, have spent a great deal in learning his profession or trade, and then receive no more pay for his labor than one who can do no more than make use of his strong arms, he would very soon say: "I have no intention whatever of connecting myself with the communistic society." The man who simply knows how to use his arms will, of course, say: "Yes, I would be made perfectly equal with the one who spent a number of years for the attainment of his proficiency in his profession or trade." If all were true Christians, they would say: "I am not working for money at all, but because God has commanded it. My daily bread I expect to receive of God, since He has given me the promise that if I labor faithfully, He will never leave me nor forsake me." The true Christian alone is of this mind. The natural man thinks, on the other hand: "Why shall I labor when there is nothing gained by it?" How many merchants say: "Why shall I keep this or that article of goods for there is no profit in it." Whether the goods are in demand or not is not the question because they are serving only themselves; —and thus we find it in every station of life. This is the selfish principle of the natural man as he is born into the world.

If, then, there is to be any help for the world, the people must become Christians, as said above. There is no other way. There are, however, many thousands of people who are called Christians, but who are not such. The communists see this and then exclaim: "What Christians? Why they are the greatest scoundrels on earth." We must admit that it is even so, that there are many scoundrels among those who bear the Christian name, who are not worthy of the name. But when we speak of Christians, we do not mean those who simply have the name, but those who do not only believe in the Bible, but who, in their life, manifest and carry out the principles contained in the Bible. These alone are Christians, and if all were such Chris tians, we would have heaven on earth, and the cross, which we must expect, would be easy to bear. Of course, no communist will believe this, because he does not know the meaning of the term Christian. He only sees the faults and sins of those who call themselves Christians and perhaps also attend church, and then exclaims: "What? Christianity shall improve the world? Are not the Christians worse than we?" And alas! we are forced to say: "O wretched communists! You are indeed fearfully offended, and woe unto him through whom this offense comes; for he hardens you and causes you to believe the more firmly that Christianity amounts to nothing. But it remains true, after all, that men are naturally selfish, and they will remain selfish until they become true Christians; it is therefore madness to think of creating a world in which everyone is satisfied to have no more than others."

We must not imagine that many who are very wealthy would be satisfied in having no more than others. To illustrate, there is a man who is worth 10,000, 100,000, 500,000, or even 1,000,000 dollars. Would he accommodate himself to such a communistic society and become a member? The communist Fourier (died 1837) attempted to carry out his communism in France and even succeeded in gathering together here and there little communistic congregations, which he called Phalanstères. There 1800 to 2000 persons lived together having all things in common. There were no rulers except the so-called distributors. For someone has to give the command: "So much belongs to you and so much to another; this is your work, and that is his." But alas! money was wanting. Fourier then published a request in the papers that some wealthy person should, out of love for mankind, contribute one million dollars for this purpose. He (Fourier) would go to a certain place every day to see whether so kind a man would come. He went to the place every day for 12 years, but no one came. All his Phalanstères became bankrupt.

These communistic gentlemen, like Fourier, are either fanatics or swindlers. We will readily believe that the leaders are mostly fanatics because, having nothing more to do with Christianity, they have asked themselves day after day: "What can we do to elevate the deeply fallen world to happiness again?" And they have devised this plan. But what can it accomplish? People are not made happy, but *un*happy by this means; and as the communists continually call the attention of the people to the dreadful condition of the world, they also more firmly fix the idea in the minds of the people: "How wretched is the world! O how unhappy! we must take another course." This is the poison with which the communists feed the people. This is the poison which is all the more dreadful in its effects, because we know that the condition of the world will remain the same. And if a thousand communistic papers would be published, they could not turn the world upside down, they cannot change the condition of the world. What do they gain, then? No more than this: that people feel that they are unhappy. If one who is poor thinks: "I am poor and cannot follow the pace set by the rich; yet I will not care, but be contented with my condition, if I can only make an honest living —he is a happy man as poor as he may be. This then brings us to our third proposition:

3. It is a fact that happiness does not consist in external advantages.

Even the communist must acknowledge that outward equality would not by any means make all men happy, because the wants of the human heart are not alike. One person is happy only in this particular position; another only in that position. He who has not yet learned these imaginary wants, has his cup of coffee, bread, and butter for breakfast; a common dinner in the presence of a faithful wife and obedient children: potato soup for his supper, and holds his family worship, does not only think himself happier than a king, —he is, in reality, a thousand times happier. Happiness does not dwell in palaces; it dwells in the heart. Though you give a person all the riches of the earth, you will not make him happy. It is a mania, with which nearly everyone is affected, to think: "If we only had as much as others, we would be happy also." Cares come with riches. Go from castle to castle, enter the rooms where princes and emperors dwell, and you will see how happy they are. You would find that if Christian faith were wanting, they are unhappy notwithstanding the power, the riches, and the honors which they enjoy. Happiness is not found in these things; we simply imagine it. Happiness depends upon the condition of the mind. And if you would fill a man's house with gold and diamonds, —that would never satisfy the heart. It has wants of a different character.

Even though we do make these statements, they are mostly made in vain, for people will not believe us. They say: "O if I only had plenty of money, I would feel right happy." They are fanatics who make such declarations. Just make an imaginary experiment with yourself, and you will find that a fearful burden is placed upon your heart by becoming the owner of a large lump of gold. Gellert beautifully presents the matter in the poem called "John, the soapmaker."[4] He speaks of a soap boiler who sang with cheerfulness day and night. He had his daily bread and performed His work gladly. A wealthy epicure lived near him. He is greatly vexed at John's disturbing him in his morning sleep. He entered into a contract with John that he would give him a thousand dollars if he would stop his singing. John said to himself: "I can well afford to stop for a thousand dollars." He carried the money home. He stopped his singing, but peace and joy fled from his heart and mind. While lying in bed, if he heard a little noise, he would think: "There are thieves about!" In short, his happiness was gone. Finally, he gathered up his money again and carried it back to his rich neighbor. He preferred to sing and be joyful. This is, of course, a fable, but it is based on the experience of millions of people. It is, then, altogether contrary to nature to try to make men happy by means of communism.

The Word of God alone can make us happy. A man may indeed succeed well in some undertaking and become overjoyed for a time and feel himself very happy. But alas! it is only for a short time! A Christian, on the other hand, is always happy, even while weeping. And if he should be prostrated before his God, he must confess, "Happy man that I am!" He knows that he has enjoyed God's goodness; he knows his tears will soon be wiped away. He will be with his God and Father and will stand before His throne forevermore when once the delusive play on the stage of life is ended. The Christian knows this, and therefore he is happy. He is, of course, not always in a pleasant mood; sometimes he feels very sad, yes, quite frequently so; and the deeper his Christianity, the more he will be troubled with feelings of sadness, inasmuch as he notices every action of his flesh. This causes him trouble and distress. However, one thing no one can take from him: he has a merciful God in heaven; he has found the precious pearl, and when life is at an end, he can cheerfully close his eyes, for he fears neither death nor hell nor that "Nothing" of which the atheists are continually afraid.

Although there are many who say: "There is no God," there are really not as many atheists, even in our times, as is generally supposed. Many a one is a very bold atheist by day, but when he retires in the evening, and all is dark about him, he hears a silent voice within him, saying: "There is a God after all; it is at any rate doubtful whether there is a God or not, and should there be a God, what will become of me?" This voice can be silenced by nothing less than satanic obduracy and hardness of heart. An atheist may deliver a speech with glowing eloquence against the existence of a God, but we must not think that he is actually in earnest. There are many braggarts who would show their intellectual greatness by speaking against God. Then after they return to their home, they must accuse themselves and say: "What have you done!" They don't believe themselves what they have said. God has written on the heart of man, and no one can erase it: "There is a God, before Him, thou wilt be called to an account. He will bring thee before His judgment seat. Woe unto thee if thou hast no Savior? He will judge thee strictly in accordance with His holiness and righteousness." —

Because, then, it is a fact that happiness does not consist in external advantages, it is folly to endeavor to make men happy by means of an equalization.

Second Lecture

O God, thou hast not created man for this short earthly life. The immortal mind of man is not bound to time and earth, like the soul of irrational animals, but lifts itself beyond all things created, even into boundless eternity. The heart of man cannot be satisfied with things temporal and earthly, like the blind instinct of animals, but it hungers and thirsts for eternal, for perfect gifts. In this present world, Thou wouldst only prepare man for his final world, Thou wouldst only prepare man for his final goal, in another world he shall attain it: here he is to sow, there he shall reap; here he is to labor, there he shall receive the reward; here he is to pass through trials, there he shall be elevated to glory; here truth and falsehood, right and oppression are to

*contend with each other, there truth and
right shall be crowned victorious.*

*O grant, then, that we may not seek our
happiness, rest, and peace in the perish-
able things of this world; we would not
find it after all. Grant also that midst
the troubles of this life, we may not
despair, but that we may be strong like
men and cheerfully engage in the
appointed contest. But above all, grant
that in these times of falling away and
infidelity, our faith in Thy Word may
not waver, that we may find comfort in
Thine only begotten Son Jesus Christ, our
Redeemer, and that we may eventually,
by His grace, depart this life in peace and
behold Thee face to face in the joys of that
eternal Day. Amen.*

————

My friends, whoever thinks that we Lutherans take no part in the agitations of the socialists and communists, but rather oppose them because we are not acquainted with the troubles of the laboring men, or because we have no sympathy for them, or because under all circumstances we side with the rich, the so-called great and rulers, is greatly in error. How could it be otherwise than that we should be well acquainted with the troubles, particularly of these times, of the laboring men? The greatest number, by far, of the members of our

Lutheran congregations are persons who are oppressed with the troubles common among the laboring men. It is an exceedingly rare occurrence, if once in a great while, a man of wealth or influence connects himself with one of our congregations. We also well know that the present great troubles which have come upon our laboring men are not by any means simply a natural necessity; the cause of the trouble is to be found somewhere else, namely, in part, yes, almost altogether, in the self-interest, avarice, and selfishness, in the cruelty and heartlessness, and. to speak plainly, in the vampirism and tyrannical oppression of the worker on the part of the rich. Let no one think that we do not sympathize with the laboring men. When we read of the heart-rending scenes which occur almost daily, particularly in the larger cities, in the shanties of the laboring men, it causes our hearts to bleed, and we are willing and ready to do our part, little as it may be, to improve the condition of the poor laboring-man. It is not true, either, that we side with the rich and influential under all circumstances. No, when the rich are unchristian in their conduct towards the poor, when they look upon them as existing simply for their profit, when they treat them as a cow is treated, which is milked and then turned into the woods, if they will not give the laborer proper wages, if they will not, when such is possible, procure for him paying labor if they will not pay for damages sustained to the laborer who has been unfortunate while in their services if they will not support the laborer and his family in case of sickness, if they can live in luxury and be unconcerned when the laborer is suffering: then we are not their friends, but, from principle their enemies!

O my brethren, what term of reproach might not be justly applied to us, if we sided with the human vampires and not with the oppressed!

We would be the most infamous and abject hypocrites under the sun, or that ever walked on the earth, if we would, notwithstanding this, pretend that the Holy Scriptures were the book of our religion. The Holy Scriptures are the very book which does not only declare that the first and greatest command is that "we love God above all things;" but also adds: "And the second is like unto it, Thou shalt love thy neighbor as thyself." It is this book which declares: "All things whatsoever ye would that men should do to you, do ye even so to them: for this is the law and the prophets," that is, this is the essence, the sum and substance, the common center of the legal part of the entire Scriptures. It is the Scriptures which cry vengeance upon the heads of the unrighteous capitalists, and which proclaim a thousandfold vengeance upon those who have capital simply to increase it, or to make themselves comfortable, who never concern themselves about their neighbors, who never think that it is because of the poor that they are rich, who, accordingly leave the poor Lazarus lying at the door of their palaces; while they are within faring sumptuously every day. No, we do not side with them. We herewith declare that we have nothing to do with them, and if socialism and communism are now causing them trouble and anxiety, it is no more than they deserve.

But, my brethren, notwithstanding this, we cannot side with the socialists or with the communists, and that principally for these reasons: They would go too far, they would accomplish more than they either can or should accomplish, and then again because they would employ means which no God-fearing man can employ. If, accordingly, the communists and socialists would equalize everything in the world, introduce the community of goods so that no one will be rich and no one poor, or if they would, in order to gain this end, shed blood, if necessary, we cannot side with them. For we know that it is God's order, that in spiritual things, i.e., things pertaining to our relation to God, we are all equal, for with God there is no respect of persons, but that in this world there must be a difference between men both as respects their possessions and their positions. Without this difference, the world could not exist. In the second place, the Scriptures teach us that the individual does not bear the sword, but this is a prerogative of the government. When the Apostle Peter would defend his Master with the sword, and for which he seemed to have a perfect right —for who was ever more shamefully and unjustly taken by violence than our Lord Jesus Christ!— Christ tells him: "Put up thy sword into the sheath, for all they that take the sword, shall perish with the sword." Even when the Lord was in the presence of Pilate, who among all rulers was the most unjust, he acknowledged: "Thou couldst have no power at all against me, except it were given thee from above." Pilate was a ruler and, by virtue of his office, had the power. Moreover, if the communists and socialists would even partly gain their desired object, they would not only have to gain it by the shedding of blood, but their glory would continue only for a short time, and they would soon see how sadly they had deceived themselves and others. This is the subject which we will now consider more in detail.—

We left off with the fourth subdivision of the first part of our essay. The first part reads: No reasonable man, much less a Christian, can take part in the efforts of the communists and socialists, much less become a member of one of their organizations, because these efforts are contrary to reason, nature, and experience. It is then said:

4. It is a fact well established by experience, that the communists never attained their professed end, and only introduced sorrow and suffering.

These beautiful whims of the Communists, relating to the future, are of no consequence; the same can be said of their representations of the golden times which will come after they have fully organized the world. History must decide. But history condemns communism. Schiller's words may well be applied here, although used by him for a godless sense: "The history of the world is the judgment of the world." There are, in reality, things which are already judged by history; to these belong these new systems, which are, however, already old.

Going back then in history, we find that the first state, which was, to a certain extent, arranged communistically, was that of the Spartans. They divided all their goods; but it is doubtful whether the communists and socialists will recognize the Spartans as their real ancestors, inasmuch as they had, in connection with their communistic arrangements, slavery, and at that a terrible slavery. So-called helots had to do the farming and carry on all trades and professions; the Spartan nobility concerned itself nothing about these things. They concerned themselves only with military affairs. The Spartan state was evidently not altogether communistic. Lycurgus gave Sparta a constitution 800 years before Christ.

Six hundred years before Christ, Pythagoras arranged his school of philosophy on the Communistic plan. But I doubt whether the communists would recognize in him a true ancestor. For no one was admitted into this society until he had abstained from speaking for a number of—and to this, the communists would hardly consent; then again, the Pythagoreans did not intend to organize the whole human race into a society on the basis of these principles, but considered these a more exalted position on which the philosopher must stand, inasmuch as he is not concerned about the earthly and visible, but only regards the idea which governs his mind.

Plato, the renowned philosopher, lived 400 years before Christ. He wrote a book treating exclusively of government and the commonwealth. In this book, he also says that the most beautiful and most perfect form of a republic is that of communism. It is remarkable, however, that he forbids only those in the higher stations of life to hold private or personal property; the people, on the other hand, were not to be organized on the principles of communism.

In speaking of an impracticable theory, it is now generally said to be a Platonic idea, or a Platonic republic. The expression occurs in the symbolical books of our Lutheran Church in the article treating of the church, in which it is said that the fanatical spirits imagined the church to be a Platonic republic, the description of which looks well on paper but can never be realized.

Two hundred years before Christ, there existed a sect

among the Jewish people called the Essenes, who also had
their possessions in common. But it was not their intention
to recommend their constitution to the whole world, as do
our communists. They did not expect that this form of
government would bring happiness to man, but on the
contrary, they would live in this manner for the very
purpose of denying themselves many things, hoping
thereby to merit something before God. It was self-right-
eousness, feigned holiness, that prompted them to this.

With reference to the early Christians, we will have
occasion to speak under the second main division, from
which we will see that the early Christians were not for
Communism as some affirm.

In the Romish church, there is a strong communistic
tendency: for every order of monks and nuns is based on
communistic principles. But our communists will hardly
recognize these either. The Romish monks and nuns also
declare that they do not enter the cloister for the purpose of
taking part in the common happiness of man, but much
rather, to withdraw themselves from the happiness of the
world, to lead a life of abstinence, that by this means they
may gain a more lofty position in heaven. These, then, do
not come into consideration here.

At the time of the Reformation, communism, as it is
now developing itself, was already in existence. The first
communist during Luther's time was Thomas Muenzer, a
Lutheran preacher, a talented man, but very fanatical.
History gives us the following account of him.

In the year 1524, there arose a Lutheran preacher in
Thuringia by the name of Thomas Muenzer; he advocated
communistic principles, which he summed up in these

words: *"omnia simul communia,"* which he circumscribed
as follows: "All things shall be common, and occasionally
they shall be distributed according to each one's necessity;
and whatever prince, count, or lord will not submit to this,
and being forewarned, his head shall be stricken off or he
shall be hung.[1]"He traveled through Germany and Switzer-
land and, executing his scheme, stirred up the flames of
sedition everywhere; returned to Thuringia, took possession of Muelhausen, had cannons cast in the Franciscan
cloister, issued a proclamation to all the princes demanding
their resignation, finally collected together 8,000 peasants,
ransacked the cloisters and the houses of the rich, and after
the peasants had rejected the offer of mercy, provided they
would deliver up the ringleaders, he gave the princes battle
at Frankenhausen, singing the hymn: "Now we pray the
Holy Spirit." He was, however, most ignominiously
defeated, his whole army destroyed, nearly 7,000 of his men
perished, and he himself was captured and put to death.
This was the beginning and the end of the first communistic movement during the time of the Reformation.

At the same time, there was a sedition raised among the
peasants in Swabia by the propagation of communistic
ideas. Luther's doctrine of Christian liberty was misunder-
stood. That which Luther had preached concerning liberty
in the kingdom of God, was also applied to the kingdom of
this world. The peasants had a preacher draw up 12 articles
which contained their demands. Among other things, they
demanded liberty in hunting, liberty in fishing, liberty in
cutting wood, deliverance from villenage, etc.; but without
waiting for the acceptance of the articles, they marched
through the land with devastation and murder, assaulted

and destroyed castles and cloisters, declaring that everything wearing spurs should die. They made a fearful slaughter and, in many instances, in a most inhuman manner. Count Lewis of Helfenstein was driven upon the spears of the peasants during the sounding of the drum and the shalm. His wife, who with her little boy cast herself upon her knees before the peasants and begged for mercy, was hauled away on a dung cart midst jeers and mockery. Many of the nobility yielded. But even a Goetz of Berlichingen, their leader, could endure the horrible crimes only 8 days. 179 castles and 28 cloisters were consumed by the flames. All of Upper Germany yielded. Finally, the princes arose against them, the result of which was that nearly 100,000 peasants perished most miserably, some in battle and some on the gallows, and their condition was made worse.

What Luther thought of this movement is evident from one of his writings, which he published on this subject. It was called "An admonition for peace, in answer to the 12 articles of the peasants." The peasants themselves had sent a request to him, asking him to give his opinion on the matter; for they had thus far seen that he severely reproved all oppression, tyranny, and injustice. They hoped that he would side with them; and, in part, Luther did side with them. In the above-named writing, he, in the first place, speaks of the princes, prelates, the great, and the rich, and shows them that, in reality, they, and no one else, were the cause of this great calamity.—This is truly a good warning to us Lutherans living at this age, that we may not suffer ourselves to be misled by the fact that the communists and socialists are doing wrong so that we would at once side with all those against whom this warfare is carried on; for truly, if righteousness and love had ruled the world, such agitations would never have been called forth. Unrighteousness is undoubtedly the source of these troubles; only this is to be condemned that they go too far and do not use the right means to improve the condition of affairs.

Luther did not flatter the princes. He was not afraid of their wrath, for he was thoroughly convinced that he was called of God, now, after the lie had triumphed so many years, to declare the truth, not only to the poorer class but also to the big Jacks, as he calls them—He continues:

"The sword is upon your necks, and yet you imagine that you are so firmly seated in the saddle that no one shall be able to lift you out. Such security and - obdurate presumption will break your necks; you will see it. I have frequently declared unto you before this, that you should take warning from the 107th Ps. v. 40: 'He poureth contempt upon princes.' You are striving for it, and want to receive a blow upon your heads, there is no use in warning and admonishing you. Be it then so, since you have caused this wrath of God, it shall undoubtedly also come upon you if you do not change your course in time . . . For this you shall know, my lords, that God so manages affairs, that your raving neither can, nor will, nor should be endured. You must change your course and yield to God's Word. If you will not do so in a cheerful and friendly way, you will be compelled to do so by force and destruction. Should these peasants not accomplish it, others must do it, and if you should kill them all, you would not be victorious. God will raise up others. For He has determined to destroy you, and He will destroy you. It is not the peasants who are contending against you; it is God himself; he is contending against you with his just retribution for your madness . . . Now then, my lords, if you will yet receive advice, for God's sake, make way somewhat for their wrath. A load of hay should avoid a drunkard's way; how much more should not you give up your raving and tyrannical obstinacy and conduct yourselves with reason towards the peasants being either in frenzy or error? Do not begin to quarrel with them, for there is no telling what the end would be. Use kindness first, for you cannot tell what God is about to do, lest a spark should begin to burn and set all Germany on fire, so that no one shall be able to quench it. Our sins have come before God, in consequence of which we are to fear this wrath, even if we but hear the rustling of a leaf, and why not when such a crowd is in commotion?"

He says: "Our sins." A true Lutheran must also count himself among those who have deserved it, when such fearful parties arise in society, who are bent on turning everything upside down and on drowning the world, excepting themselves, in its own blood. It is a divine judgment of the world. —Luther continues:

"By kindness you lose nothing; and if you should lose anything, it can be restored to you again in time of peace tenfold whereas by strife you may lose life and property . . . They have set up 12 articles, some of which are so just and right that they expose your lack of kindness before God and the world and verify the 107th Psalm, inasmuch as they are pouring contempt upon the princes. But nearly all of these articles were set up professedly for their special benefit and advantage and are really not intended for their good. I might write other articles against you, with reference to the community and government of Germany, as I did in the book to the German nobility, which would be of even more importance than the latter."

He would say: "Principles which care nothing if the rest of the world perish if only help is procured for one particular station in life, can only work injury in the world." Luther says: "While considering the misery and distress of Germany, even in civil matters, I also had thought of giving advice for the improvement of every station of life, and not only for the clerical in which I stood,—if there is actually such a station." He continues:

"But because you would not take warning, you must needs hear and endure such articles, and it is no, more than you have deserved for disregarding the warning. The first article, in which they desire to hear the gospel, and to have the right of electing their own pastors, you can in no way refuse . . ."

At that time, Luther made these declarations to the counts and princes, and even today, the people in most parts of Germany have no right to call their own pastors: this is done by the consistory, or the princes or the nobility; and the unfortunate people must be satisfied with anyone who may be on good terms with the princes, of whom they can expect that he will rebuke only the sins of the people, but not those of the great. Luther says further:

"No government can or should be opposed to this. A government should not oppose anything that is taught or believed, whether it be the gospel or falsehood; it is enough if they oppose the teaching of sedition and dissension."

The brethren can clearly see from this that Luther was thoroughly in favor of religious liberty. The government shall not oppose the preaching of anything, whether it be gospel or eternal life, but simply for her earthly welfare. It has no right to dictate to anyone what he shall believe, neither what he shall teach or preach.

"The other articles," Luther continues, "pertaining to oppressive taxation, as exercised in the escheats, impositions, and the like, are no more than just and right. For the government was not instituted that the rulers might be benefited and live in luxury at the expense of the subject, but that they may seek the public welfare. This extortion cannot be endured very long; of what benefit would it be to the peasant if his land would produce as many florins as straws and grains, when the rulers only take the more that they may increase their luxury and waste the goods like chaff, in dress, in banqueting, drinking, building and the like! This pomp must be put away, these expenses stopped, if the poor are to retain anything . . . My lords, you have the Scriptures and history against you. See how the tyrants seldom died a natural death, but were generally put to death and perished in their own blood. Since, then, it is certain that you rule in tyranny and recklessness and that you rob and crush the poor, you can have no other prospect than that you shall perish as those of your character have perished before you . . . I would then, with all faithfulness, advise that several counts and lords be selected from the nobility, that several councilmen be chosen from the cities, and that the matter be attended to and peaceably composed, that you cool down your rage,—this you will be compelled to do finally whether you desire it or not—at least relax your tyranny and oppression that the poor may also breathe freely. The peasants should also be advised to give up and pass by several articles which ask too much; so that the matter might then be composed, if not in a Christian manner, at least in accordance with human rights and forbearance."[2]

This rebuke and admonition of the princes and the great who lived in his time is the beginning of Luther's address. These quotations cover only a small portion of it. Then he also speaks plainly to the peasants, showing them in particular, that they have no right to call themselves Christians if they would overcome violence with violence, and take up the sword, to which God had given them no right. Otherwise, he yields to their position in many things.

This was in 1524 and '25. Ten years later there was a similar movement in Muenster, in Westphalia, at which place the Anabaptists were forming a conspiracy. A certain tailor, John Bockhold of Leyden, declared himself king, and Mathiesson, a baker of Harlem, became his minister. They made sad work. It is revolting to give an account of the association. Things were carried on so shamefully that it seemed the devil was celebrating his wedding. Among other things, they also introduced the community of wives. These doings came to a most fearful end on the 24th and 25th of June, 1535. Although these people continued in Muenster for some time, they were finally driven out of their nest, the majority of them were most unmercifully slaughtered, and the prisoners cruelly put to death. Such was the beginning and such the end of these communistic movements.

From this time up to the time of the first French Revolution, which lasted from 1789 to 1797, there were no developments of the communistic theory worth mentioning. While the leaders of the first revolution in France, the "Jacobins," still recognized the right of personal property, a certain Babeuf formed a communistic conspiracy with the downfall of Robespierre. The following was his doctrine: "Every individual has the same right to make use of all goods, which right is based on common labor. Every exclusive appropriation of products of the soil and industries is criminal." Besides, some of the members declared that the necessary equality required "the destruction of aristocratic cities, the prevention of inequality in knowledge and education and the establishment of a censorship for the preservation of permanent relations."

Do not imagine, then, that communist ideas, if carried out, would introduce liberty. They would much rather bring about the most horrid slavery imaginable. For the holding of personal property, which the communists condemn, is the very condition on which a man may freely develop and exercise himself. However, as soon as a communist state would be established, everyone would receive his orders: "This is what you have to do, you will do so much, and you so much." They would then be as the helots among the Spartans. Should a person, however, have been in want for a long time, even of his daily bread, and would then get among the communists and sit down to a loaded table, he would, of course, think he had entered heaven. It would not continue long, however, until he would say: "May God preserve me against such a condition of affairs. Let me be liberated from this slavery!" And the censorship is a similar slavery. But no one is more bitterly opposed to it than the communists. It is something dreadful to them; the very word is dreadful to them. And yet whenever they obtained the power, they introduced a most stringent censorship; for they have always feared that if their principles should be found open to objection with the poor and uneducated, these people would begin to doubt their correctness, and their reign would again be overthrown. —Babeuf's principles are further stated as follows:

"The only rulers should be a board of distributors, whose duty it shall be to appoint each one to his labor and to distribute to the communities and individuals the provisions gathered into the public warehouses. A higher Being is to be recognized, but no Church, no priest, no marriage, and no family." The conspiracy was discovered and called to account; Babeuf permitted himself to be stabbed, some of the others were beheaded, some burned. This was in the year 1796.

This closed the first communist movement during the first revolution in France. The next movement began during the first thirty years of the nineteenth century. After the so-called July Revolution, new Babeufs arose in France. The strictest among them called themselves Egaliteurs, who declared that they would make all things equal, advocated not only the abrogation of personal property, but also of marriage and family life, and proclaimed Atheism. In consequence of a revolt, they were divided in the year 1839 and thereby lost the influence they had in the beginning. But the seed remained in the hearts of the people and is at present taking root. Now a word regarding other communists of this century.

Count de Saint-Simon (who committed suicide in 1825 after he had lost all his property and had been driven into dire necessity) proclaimed the following theories to the world: "The laboring class must be elevated to the highest position of human society because they furnish the means by which man's desires and wants are satisfied, while at present they unjustly occupy the lowest. The self-sacrificing love of all alone makes this possible. This doctrine is the new Christianity, which will introduce the kingdom of God into the world, inasmuch as it converts the religion of love into a religion of joy and pleasure." His pupil Bazard added to this: "Labor must be freed from the slavery of capital, instead of the individual inheritance, the State alone shall have the right of inheritance, and the State must divide this inheritance according to the principle that labor alone is entitled to possession, that everyone shall labor according to his ability and that everyone be rewarded according to his labor." Enfantin called Saint-Simon the new Messiah, who combined the doctrines of Moses and Christ in demanding the sanctifying of one's self by means of labor and enjoyment. All things in man are holy, the flesh with its inherent inclinations as well as the spirit. Extensive holy families are to be established in which community of wives shall also exist. This caused a division and, finally, the entire overthrow of Saint-Simonism.

It is not enough to tell people: "You must love each other, and if you walk in love, heaven will be established on earth." As true as it is that such would be the case, so true is it that no one will have love as a consequence of this demand. Love is implanted into the heart by the grace of God alone. Those who know not the grace of God and will not accept it, but despise it and tread it under foot, have no love, though their deeds should often appear as if they were deeds of love.

After the overthrow of Louis Phillipp during the revolution of February 1848, a communist insurrection broke out in Paris on the 23rd of June. A rabble of more than 30,000 took to arms; laborers from the national workhouses and escaped criminals, led by discharged officers or by the leaders of the communist clubs, constituted this rabble. Barricades were erected in the eastern part of the city. The socialist republic aimed to introduce the community of goods and of wives. On several flags was inscribed: "If victorious, we plunder; if conquered, we burn." Bishop Affre of Paris admonished them to peace but was shot on a barricade. A furious struggle ensued. Women poured boiling water and oil from the barricades upon the soldiers. On the 26th of June, Cavaignac became victorious. There were 5,000 dead and wounded on both sides; 14,000 were taken captive, of which 3,423 were transported. Louis Blanc was the instigator of the trouble.

The actual pioneers of Communism in Germany were the representatives of the so-called "Young-Germany; at the head of whom we find the noted poet Heine, and next to him were the novel writers Mund and Gutzkow. They declared that the rehabilitation of the flesh, as they termed it, must, at last, be carried out, i.e., the flesh of man must have its former rights restored. To express this intelligibly, man must again have the right to gluttonize, to drink to excess, to carry on fornication, to commit adultery, and, in short, to do everything that the flesh might desire. I am not exaggerating the matter; it is even so. Those persons mentioned above announced such principles, even if they did not express themselves so rudely; for if they had used such coarse language, they would not have been able to entangle the inexperienced youth. When I was a student at

Leipzig, they were in their glory. They are little noticed now. But the seed sown by them is now growing and bearing fruit. —Now a few words about the German Communists.

A certain Weitling, a tailor's apprentice in Magdeburg, but a very talented young man (in America he would be called a self-made man) had never attended an academy or university, and yet had acquired a good education. This Weitling describes the introduction of the new order of things, as he would have them, in the following words:

"All promissory notes, bonds, and exchange shall be null and void in the transactions of the board of directors. The same holds good with regard to inheritance . . . Consequently, every difference between poor and rich, between the low and the high, between the greatest statesmen and their lowest servants, between the highest officers and the lowest soldiers, shall be forever abolished . . . All the gold and silver in hand shall be used in purchasing provisions and ammunition in foreign lands. Money shall not be used in the inland trade. (Only a few days ago, the "Volksstimme" of this place partially expressed the same idea as the idea of the editor.) "All government and church property shall be appropriated for the good of the society. The religious instruction in the schools must be of a general character, favoring neither Catholicism nor Protestantism nor any other of the many Christian sects."[3]

He wrote this in 1842. At that time he did not yet venture fully to express his meaning; for if he had really done this, he would have had to say: "We want no particular religion, but only a universal religion, the natural religion,

just as we find it in America in the non-religious free
schools."

Of a similar character was Ferdinand Lassalle, a highly
gifted and finely educated Jew of Breslau, who wrote many
ingenious works in justification of the communist theories.
Although yet young, he was killed in a duel with a rival in
1869. But before going further, we must hear more from
our German Weitling. In his book: "Garantien der
Harmonie und Freiheit"[4] (1842), he writes:

"If I did not want the natural equality of all, I would say
with many others: Our principle will be realized alone in
the way of progressive enlightenment. Yea, all good may be
realized in this way, except the abrogation of the personal
interests of all those in possession of power and money.
When have such listened to reason? If you doubt it, ask
history. Their papers are filled with numberless accounts of
struggles between personal interests and the general interests of the People. By wars and revolutions, dynasties have
changed, obtained power, and strengthened themselves.
Our principle will be realized by means of revolution. The
longer the present confusion shall continue, the more
dreadful will be the result of such a revolution . . . In time
of peace, let us instruct, and in time of trouble, let us act.
When once the storm is raging, it is folly to waste precious
time with speeching, as was done once at Hambach, but we
must act quick as lightning, strike blow upon blow, while
the people are yet in the first stages of excitement . . ."

Very prudent indeed. As long as the people are drunk
with excitement, something can be done. But as soon as
they take a second thought, they become sober and will
then no longer follow their wild and fanatical leaders into

the fire, endangering their own lives for the destruction of thousands of other lives.

Weitling continues: "No armistice, no stipulations with the enemies can be entered into, and no promise shall be trusted. As soon as the struggle begins, they must be considered no better than irrational brutes, who are not capable of understanding a rational language."

In other words, he says: "We will either send a bullet through our opponents' heads or hang them on the nearest lamppost, for they will not learn to be rational; they will never say that we are right, and give us their money that we may divide it."

He further states: "Should those in power, in opposition to the realization of our principle, endeavor to confine us in prison, our philosophers must then let loose that fearful fireship which alone can destroy the plans of our enemies.

"He holds in reserve an instrument, even if all the agitators ventured to preach a morality which will make every government for selfish ends impossible, a morality which will convert the gory battlefield on the street, where the people have always fallen short, into a never-ceasing guerrilla war, a morality which will add to us countless numbers of defenders whose assistance we would dread at present . . ."

He means to say: "A morality must be preached by means of which those will then be added to our number, to assist us in our undertaking, whom we at present dread because of their immorality and filthiness; for their principle is: Rob, steal, plunder, murder." Therefore he continues.

"A. morality, which leaves our opponents no way of escape, than by the adoption of our principle . . . This morality can, however, only be instilled into the minds of the masses of those people found in our large cities who have fallen into the depth of misery and have become the victims of despair."[5]

When Weitling recommended those allies from among the criminals to the French communists, they manifested a little more soberness. They answered him:

"Imagine yourself at the head of 10,000 scoundrels, the time for action being at hand. Call upon your assistants to place their body upon the altar of reason and justice, that the system of community may be begun! How you would be ridiculed!"

The other evening I already referred to a certain French writer by the name of Fourier, the clerk of a merchant in France. Fourier was unfortunate and lost his valuable possessions. Before he died in 1837, he set up the following communistic theory:

"Man's destiny is happiness. This he can attain only by harmoniously satisfying all his inclinations."

But friend Fourier overlooked the fact; that man is by nature desirous of power, avaricious, envious, rejoices at the misfortune of others, revengeful, cruel, etc. Must also all these inclinations have their way? He says further:

"Means are necessary to this end. Wealth is, accordingly, the source of all happiness. Wealth is attained by means of labor. But in order that labor may produce happiness, an order of things must be introduced according to which all work together and in such a manner that each one engages in the work in which he delights. In order that this may be accomplished, the individual must be persuaded to give his possessions into the hands of the society, for which he would then have a proportionate claim on the income of the whole; and these persons, thus united, will then also give up their separate homes, families, and training."

What, accordingly, is the man entering into this communist society to give up? In the first place, he must give up his possessions even if he has acquired them ever so lawfully by means of hard labor. Then he shall give up his home and, in company with many others, move into a large building. He is to give up his marriage, and, accordingly, his family and the training of his own children. His wife is not his own, but is the property of the society. Neither are his children his own. As soon as they are born, someone appointed for this purpose will take them into care and train them. I ask: Could a theory be more insane than this? Would it not be necessary for a person to have become bankrupt in every respect and despair of everything before he could enter into such an organization? If a person had yet any hope at all for the future, would he connect himself with the communists? Truly not! What greater happiness can the earth afford than that of the family? And this is to be sacrificed? —Fourier gives on:

"They form clubs or phalanxes (a square mile of land was to be the tract of land on which a phalanx or phalanstery was to be erected) consisting of 1800 to 2000 persons, who are collected in a large house, the phalanstery, where everyone finds work according to his inclination."

As already stated, in putting his theory into practice, he failed. Mr. Fourier went for 12 years to a certain place, to which he had requested any philanthropist to come and bring a million dollars for his use in the endeavor to realize his glorious theory. Fourier's pupil, Victor Considerant, conducted the phalanstery established on a large tract of land. But the undertaking was a failure. Being accused of high treason, he left for Texas.[6] What has become of him, I cannot say.[7]

Lawyer Étienne Cabet was another French communist. He founded a party called the "Icarian Communists." He died here in St. Louis. It was a strange self-ridicule to call his communism the Icarian communism. In the Greek fables, we read of a certain Icarus whose father had made him wings and had cemented them with wax, that he might escape with him from bondage and fly across the sea. The fable declares that the father reached the opposite shore in safety but that the son was too bold, flew too high, and getting too near the sun, the wax melted, and he fell into the sea and was drowned. Very strange that Cabet should call his followers the Icarian communists. They were Icarian, however, for they flew up high but had wings cemented together with wax, which would not hold.

Cabet, however, recognized the family and marriage relation and hoped to secure liberty for the so-called proletariat without using force, by means of equal training, labor, order, and above all, brotherly love. He made an attempt in Texas in 1848 but utterly failed; the colonists sued him for fraud, but he was declared not guilty. He then made a second attempt in Nauvoo, Illinois, where the Mormons formerly had their home; he failed again. The colony was again dissatisfied. Cabet had to flee to St. Louis, where he died in 1856.

Proudhon proclaimed as his principle: "The holding of

property is theft; God is the evil; marriage and the family are unnecessary." He died in 1865.

History brings us yet to the last communist movement in France in 1871. The capitulation of the Parisians to the German besiegers gave the Internationals an opportunity to take possession of the city. Generals Lecomte and Thomas, who had remained faithful to the government, were caught on the 18th of March 1871 and shot that very afternoon. The leader of the national guard, Blanqui, a zealous International, now ordered an election for a so-called "Commune," i.e., for an independent board of directors of the city of Paris. His plan, as well as that of his associates, was to divide the whole of France into "communes," that is, small independent districts, which should have their own administration of justice and, all combined, should form a French confederacy.

An officer bearing a flag of truce was shot down. Church property was confiscated. The laborers took possession of the factories from which the owners had fled. Archbishop Darboy and other prelates and priests were put to death, and a stringent censorship instituted. The Commune even excelled Robespierre's reign of terror. "War against the palaces" was their watchword. A corps of "rocket-men," associated with male and female incendiaries, called *petroleurs* and *petroleuses*, was formed. Persons of high rank were seized and held as hostages. For an entire week, the most inhuman and most frightful scenes of fratricidal massacre took place on the streets. 794 of Mac Mahon's soldiers were killed, and 6,000 wounded. It is difficult to ascertain how many of the Internationals perished, but the number would evidently reach thousands. To conclude, the leaders of the Commune were arrested and tried for life: the most notorious were banished; officers who had deserted were executed.

This is then the history of communism in its main features. What have the communists accomplished? — Nothing! — They have hurled themselves into indescribable misery, filled the world with dread and apprehension, and continually caused destruction, misery, and heart-rending woe. And just as they have been unable to accomplish anything in the past, they will not accomplish anything in the future. The communists will be no more able to realize their fanatical ideas in human society than they will be able to change the laws of nature or cause the Mississippi to flow northward, or change the course of the stars. It is, however, apparent that they will do a great deal of mischief. For the number of the poor is continually increasing, many of whom neither believe in God nor in His Word, in consequence of which they soon despair when in trouble, having no God and no comfort. These the theoretical communists would combine, and notwithstanding the fact that they have been repeatedly conquered, they would resume their efforts, but only to be again brought under judgment and to be hurled into unspeakable wretchedness.[8][9]

Third Lecture

"O Lord, how great and how manifold are
Thy works! In wisdom hast Thou made
them all, the earth is full of Thy riches."
Such was the language of Thy servant
David thousands of years ago, after
meditating over the works of Thy
creation, preservation and government.
We at the present can but repeat this
exclamation with Thy servant David,
for wherever we turn our eyes, we behold
bright and shining traces of Thy endless
power, wisdom and goodness.
O preserve Thou us then against that spirit of
darkness, which calls itself light, and
which is at present poured out upon
myriads of unhappy people, which denies
Thee the Creator, Preserver and Ruler of
all things, or at least maliciously subverts

Thy sacred administration and wisely
arranged order of things.
Enable us rather, ever more to acknowledge
that Thou doest all things well, and that
sinful man alone has corrupted Thy
work. Grant therefore, that, as often as
the troubles of earth lie heavily upon us,
we may reprove ourselves and not Thee.
Let us not perish in the rising floods of
unbelief, and although thousands and
tens of thousands should fall from Thee,
help Thou us, that we may continue in
the faith to our end, when our faith shall
be changed into vision, and our hope into
enjoyment. Hear us for the sake of Jesus
Christ, Thine only begotten Son, our
Lord and Savior. Amen.

———

All of you here tonight well know the question for our consideration this evening, to wit: Why should and can no reasonable man, much less a Christian, take part in the efforts of communists and socialists? To this question, three answers are given:

I. Because their efforts are contrary to reason, nature, and experience;
II. because these efforts are contrary to Christianity, and finally
III. because the charges of communism against the Church

and the Christian religion that they rather hinder than promote the material welfare of man are confounded and unjust.

The first answer has been considered. We have tested communism by reason, nature, and history and have seen that it does not stand even these tests. But there have even been Christians, who have claimed that communism and socialism could also be justified by the Holy Scriptures, the only true source of Christianity. Yes, unbelievers have made this claim, some of them communists; of course, the latter did so, not because they themselves believed it, but that they might use our own weapons against us Christians.

There are particularly four passages of the Holy Scriptures which are adduced to show us that if we would faithfully adhere to the Bible, we must necessarily also justify the efforts of the communists and socialists. The first passage is found in the first chapter of the Holy Scriptures, where God gives man authority over the earth and all things in the earth. The second is found in the fourth and fifth chapters of Acts, where the condition of the first Christian congregation at Jerusalem is presented. The third passage is found in the 18th chapter of St. Luke, where an account is given of Christ saying to a rich man: "Sell all that thou hast, and distribute unto the poor, and thou shalt have treasure in heaven; and come, follow me." The fourth passage is found in the 20th chapter of the Gospel according to St. Matthew. At this place, we have a record of the familiar parable of the laborers in the vineyard.

We will, accordingly, in the first place, closely examine these portions of Scripture and become convinced whether

these are really for or against communism and socialism,
i.e., for or against the community of goods or common
labor with a common profit.

We read in the first chapter of Genesis: "Let us make
man in our image, after our likeness, and let them have
dominion over the fish of the sea, and over the fowl of the
air, and over the cattle, and over all the earth, and over every
creeping thing, that creepeth upon the earth. So God
created man in his own image . . . , and said unto them . . .
replenish the earth and subdue it; and have dominion over
the fish of the sea, and over the fowl of the air, and over
every living thing that moveth upon the earth . . . And God
said: behold I have given you every herb bearing seed, which
is upon the face of all the earth and every tree, in the which
is the fruit of a tree yielding seed; to you it shall be for
meat." From this, it is true, we learn that God has given to
the human race the earth, together with all things that live
and move on the earth, as their possession. But we do not
learn from this, how the possessions of the entire human
race are to be used, nor in what manner the earth and all
things that live and move upon the earth shall be used. God
must accordingly have left the arrangement of these things
to man himself, that is, to his reason. If a rich man would
give to a carpenter, who had been unfortunate and had
been sold out, a saw, a plane and other tools, bread, meat,
coffee, a sewing machine, a doll, a hobby horse, and other
play-things, he would have presented these things to the
entire family of the poor carpenter; and if he gave no direc-
tions, how these things should be used and appropriated,
the carpenter would know that all these things, presented to
him and his family, were to be disposed of according to his

good judgment. The carpenter would know that the hobby horse and the other play-things were not intended for him but for his children, and if he had received a cradle, he would well know that it was not intended for him to lie in. Nor would he think that the sewing machine was for him but for his wife. In short, these possessions would be for the family and were to be divided among the members of it. God's doings have been similar. The whole earth and all things therein he has given to man, but he has not determined how man shall use them. Man is no brute, without reason and without a knowledge of the aim of life. Man has reason, and this he is to use. It is self-evident that at the beginning, when there were no owners on the whole earth, so far as the individual is concerned, everyone could appropriate to himself whatever he desired. Whatever he appropriated was his own. The same would hold good even at the present day. If, for example, a crew should be ship-wrecked and would be driven to an uninhabited island owned by no one, the crew would simply take possession of the island. Everyone would have the right to settle down and appropriate a certain portion of the island to himself.

But what was done after God the Lord had given the earth, and all things on the earth, to the entire human race? Did perhaps the people in the earliest times institute communism, community of goods, or common labor with a common profit? In the fourth chapter of Genesis we read: "And Abel was a keeper of sheep, but Cain was a tiller of the ground. And in process of time it came to pass, that Cain brought of the fruit of the ground an offering unto the Lord. And Abel, he also brought of the firstlings of his flock, and of the fat thereof." We see accordingly that Abel was a keeper of sheep and carried on breeding of cattle, and that Cain was a farmer, and that each one offered unto the Lord of that which he possessed. Neither Cain nor Abel considered his own the common property of both, but each one offered that which he could justly call his own personal property. Otherwise, he could not have presented it as his offering.

We see accordingly that reason already taught the first persons living on the earth that the holding of personal property was a necessity among men for the reason that without the holding of personal property, neither peace nor unity could be preserved. The communist Fourier indeed said that in his communist republic, everyone should have whatever he needed, and everyone should engage in that work for which he was particularly inclined. But it must be remembered that enjoyments are so altogether different. There is good wine produced and also poor wine. There are a great many poor fruits and few that are extra good. Now who would say: "I will take the poor wine?" Who would say: "I will ride the poor horse?" Who would say: "I will do the meanest kind of drudgery?" Everyone would want to engage in the best and the easiest and the most honorable work, and peace would soon be at an end. Just as necessary then as concord and peace are to the human race, so necessary is the holding of personal property.

To this, we must yet add: Reason further requires the holding of personal property because there dwells in the natural man a certain desire for liberty and independence. If man is not in a measure free and independent, he cannot be happy. Take away personal property, and you put an end to liberty. Others would then prescribe to him what he should do, how he should live, what he should eat and drink, where he should live, and where he should be employed. Truly, I would not stay in a society where I had not perfect liberty in self-determination. I would as soon live under the Russian knout, under the police of China, or the despotism of Turkey. For I would then at least be conscious of the fact that I was forced to it in opposition to my will—and here shall I willingly subject myself to all this? Never, no, never! For this reason, Cain, when society became oppressive to him after he had committed murder, left and went into another land and there built a city for himself and family, and called it Enoch.

A modern writer gives a graphic description of the wretched condition which a communist must realize in a communist state. He says: "'La loi' (i.e., law or command) plans and tells the 50 millions of Icarians all they shall do and all they shall leave undone. La loi fixes the time for labor at so many hours and so many minutes; la loi prescribes to the young ladies and gentlemen when and how long they shall make their toilet; la loi introduces a 'new dish of vegetables' into every Icarian family; la loi provides for cold meat at the Icarian picnics; la loi commands, similar to Babeuf's communist state, that all literature not officially recognized, shall be burned as worthless literature," etc.[1]

This is no exaggeration. It is indeed true that the communists do not imagine that such would be the state of affairs if their ideas were realized. They will say: "This is all false; we do not think of establishing such a state. We are free people, and we will provide that in such a communist state we shall not sacrifice our liberty." But they may say what they please, and they may twist themselves as they please: whoever accepts the principle, must also accept the deduction, and that is, that man loses his personal liberty; for this is based, as stated, above all things, on the holding of personal property; and on this, that in accordance with my ability, I can choose the service that I would perform, as well as the calling in which I would labor. I must have liberty to leave my position again; I must have liberty to do with my own as I see fit. All this is denied to me the moment I enter into a communist society. For just as soon as such liberty is granted, the principle on which communism is based would be destroyed.

The third reason why the people of the earliest times already knew from reason that the holding of personal property was essential to earthly happiness is this: if no one held any personal property, that incentive, which almost everyone needs, if he would exert himself and do his work well, would be wanting. Why do many persons work from morning till night? Because they would gain something by it. This is, of course, not the right motive. Christians should not be induced to labor diligently by the desire to gain something, but they should labor for God's sake because of God's order and command. But nearly everyone labors exclusively for gain; some perhaps not just for money and goods, but then it is for honor, respect, and fame. This incentive is taken from man just as soon as he ceases to hold personal property.

The first generation of men was further induced to assert the claim of personal property by an intuitive perception of equity. This dictates to everyone that the pay shall be according to the work done. Diligent, faithful, and successful labor should be more liberally rewarded. But just as soon as men enter into a society in which the profit of united labor belongs to all, that true equality which justice demands is at an end.

And besides, what would become of the arts and sciences in a communist state? If, for example, one would apply himself to astronomy, or philosophy, or even to theology or architecture, or painting, many would look upon him as an idler. And why? Because he would earn no money for the society by his art of science. The arts and sciences would undoubtedly be banished from the truly communist state.[2]

Every man has certain religious wants. While many of them would know nothing of religion, others have a certain impulse to serve God. The communists say, "In our communist State, no religion shall be found, and above all, we will not tolerate any religious teachers; they will be excluded." But of what benefit is it to them to pass such resolutions? They will never be able to banish the religious wants from human nature, even if man should hear nothing of God from his youth up. Even if in such a state God had never been mentioned. Conscience would wake up at any rate. But the communist state would supply no means for the building of churches and the support of preachers of the gospel.

These, then, are the various reasons why our first ancestors did not introduce the community of goods but divided all the property among themselves and thus introduced the holding of personal property, although God had given the human race the whole earth and all things on the earth.

It is even true that there are great dangers and great evils connected with the holding of personal property, as we are compelled to see it daily displayed. But here, the government should take steps to prevent a few from appropriating everything to themselves. This sin is also most earnestly rebuked in the Holy Scriptures. We read, for example, in the book of Isaiah 5:8, "Woe unto them that join house to house, field to field, till there be no place, that they may be placed alone in the midst of the earth!" It is, of course, aggravating to see how a few are buying up all the land and thereby increase its value. It is well known that the railroad companies have received, as a donation, millions of acres of land which belonged to the United States, that they might carry out their projects. This is scandalous. For if a poor man would now buy good land, he can no longer buy it at the low rate for which he could have bought it formerly from the government. This may suffice as regards the first Scripture passage cited to justify communism.

The second is found, as stated, in Acts 4:32ff. We read: "And the multitude of them that believed were of one heart, and of one soul: neither said any of them that aught of the things which he possessed was his own, but they had all things common. And with great power gave the apostles witness of the resurrection of the Lord Jesus: and grace was upon them all. Neither was there any among them that lacked: for as many as were possessors of lands or houses sold them, and brought the prices of the things that were sold, and laid them down at the apostles' feet: and distribution was made unto every man according as he had need. And Joses, who by the apostles was surnamed Barnabas (which is, being interpreted, the son of consolation), a Levite, and of the country of Cyprus, having land, sold it and brought the money and laid it at the "apostles' feet." This is certainly a glorious example of the ardent love of the early Christians. It must be remembered that at that time, too, only a few rich people accepted Christianity; the greater number of those who became Christians were poor. To this must be added the fact that no Christian's life was safe even for a single hour. The drawn sword of a blood-thirsty Herod threatened the life of every Christian. During that time of great trouble, the Christians bound themselves most intimately together, and so that no one might be in want, those of more means than others sold their real estate and placed the proceeds into a common treasury.

Thus far, it seems as if these examples really favored communism. We read, however, of no other Christian congregation of the apostolic age in which such an order of things was instituted. And furthermore, we read in Acts 5:1ff., "But a certain man" (Luke thus continues) "named Ananias, with Sapphira, his wife, sold a posses-sion, and kept back part of the price (his wife also being privy to it) and brought a certain part, and laid it "at the apostles' feet." This Ananias also wanted to be looked upon as a loving, benevolent, and merciful Christian man. To this end, he sold his possessions but kept back part of the price and brought the rest to the apostle Peter under the pretense that this was the entire sum that he had real-ized. "But Peter said, Ananias, why hath Satan filled thine heart to lie to the Holy Ghost, and to keep back part of the price of the land? While it remained, was it not thine own? and after it was sold, was it, not in thine own power?" It is particularly worthy of note that Peter here says: "While it remained, was it not thine own?" We see

from this that the first Christian congregation at
Jerusalem had not instituted such an order of things that
each one would have been compelled to give up his possessions, but the Christians did this without restraint, from
free choice. For Peter here testifies to Ananias: "It would
not have been wrong for you to keep your house and
land." Yes, he even adds: "And after it was sold, was it not
in thine own power?" "Thou couldst have said: I will give
one-half, and all would have been well; no one could have
made it a matter of conscience. The reason why it is such a
shameful deed is because thou wouldst be considered a
loving and benevolent Christian, whereas thou hast done
secretly just the contrary to what thou pretendest to have
done." We read also that the members of the first Christian congregations had houses and possessions, for example, Simon, the tanner in Joppa (Act 10:6), the wealthy
seller of purple, Lydia in Philippi (Acts 16:14, 15), then
even the deacon or almoner Philip in Jerusalem had a
house in Cesarea (Acts 21:8) and even the mother of
John, whose surname was Mark, owned a house in
Jerusalem, (Acts 12:12.)

From this, we must necessarily conclude that the first
congregation at Jerusalem was not organized according to
communist principles but that the described condition of
affairs was but an unrestrained manifestation of their love in
times of extreme necessity. After this, we read Acts 9:31,
"Then had the churches rest throughout all Judea, and
Galilee, and Samaria, and were edified: and walking in the
fear of the Lord, and in the comfort of the Holy Ghost,
were multiplied." From this time forth, this arrangement of
having in a certain measure all things common ceased in

Jerusalem. It continued for a short time only, until after the conversion of Paul about the year 36.

But what we do learn from this example is this: how a true Christian should be disposed. In his heart, IF RIGHTLY UNDERSTOOD, every Christian should be a communist. In other words, a Christian should always be ready and willing to give up all he has for the benefit of his suffering brethren whenever their necessity requires it. The apostle John accordingly says: "But whoso hath this world's good, and seeth his brother have need, and shutteth up his bowels of compassion from him, how dwelleth the love of God in him?" (1 John 3:17) The Saviour expressly declares: "Give to him that asketh thee, and from him that would borrow of thee, turn not thou away." (Matthew 5:42.) The apostle Paul commands the Christian to "labor working with his hands the thing which is good, that he may have to give to him that needeth." (Ephesians 4:28.) He does not command him to labor, working with his hands the thing which is good, that he may obtain capital and become rich, but "That he may have to give to him that needeth." The apostle Paul further says: and they that buy, as though they possessed not." (1 Corinthians 7:30.) He that owns property should then be as if he possessed nothing; his heart should not be attached to it; it should create no inward struggle to give up his possessions when his neighbor is in want or the glory of God requires it. That person is no Christian whose heart and money are one. Christ accordingly declares in the very beginning of his sermon on the mount: "Blessed are the poor in spirit; for theirs is the kingdom of heaven." What does this mean? Blessed are those, whether they have few or many possessions, who are poor in spirit. He is to be poor in his heart and mind. That man who has riches which have really become riches to him, his most precious treasure, which he secures and would not lose for the whole world, that man has not yet learned the first words of Christ's sermon on the mount: "Blessed are the poor in spirit." And if you were very rich, you should be poor in spirit; you should be as if you had none of those things which have fallen to your lot. The Psalmist therefore also says: "If riches increase, set not your heart upon them." (Psalm 62:10.)

We shall proceed further. A third passage adduced in defense of communism is Matthew 19:16 ff. (compare Luke 18:18ff.): "And behold one came and said unto him, Good Master, what good thing shall I do that I may have eternal life And he said unto him, Why callest thou me good? there is none good, but one, that is, God: but if thou wilt enter into life, keep the commandments. He saith unto him, Which? Jesus said, Thou shalt do no murder, Thou shalt not commit adultery, Thou shalt not steal, Thou shalt not bear false witness, Honor thy father and thy mother: and thou shalt love thy neighbor as thyself. The young man said unto him, All these things have I kept from my youth up: what lack I yet? Jesus said unto him, If thou wilt be perfect, go and sell that thou hast, and give to the poor, and thou shalt have treasure in heaven: and come and follow me. But when the young man heard that saying, he went away sorrowful: for he had great possessions. Then said Jesus unto his disciples, Verily I say unto you, That a rich man shall hardly enter into the kingdom of heaven. And again I say unto you, It is easier for a camel to go through the eye of a needle, than for a rich man to enter into the kingdom of

God. When his disciples heard it, they were exceedingly amazed, saying, Who then can be saved?"

When the communists hear this passage, they say: "Here you see it, here Christ has plainly told the rich what they shall do: they are to sell what they have and give to the poor." They make a logical mistake, as is evident. They make the mistake which in the art of logic is called in Latin: "*Fallacia a particulari ad universale*," i.e., a fallacy from the particular to the universal. It is, for example, stated in Scripture that Christ Jesus commanded his disciples: "Go ye into all the world and teach all nations, baptizing them in the name of the Father, and of the Son, and of the Holy Ghost" Would it not be folly to conclude: "Here you see it, that Christ commands all Christians to go into the world and to preach the gospel?" Christ says to those who had been healed: "Go show yourself unto the priests." Would it not be extreme folly to conclude from this that all must show themselves to the priests? But it is just as foolish to attempt to show that it is Christ's doctrine that all the rich must sell all their possessions and give to the poor, from Christ's command to the rich young man: "Sell that thou hast."

Why, then, did Christ address these words to the rich young man? The answer is at hand. This rich man was a ruler, a counselor, who imagined that he had fulfilled all the commandments of God. But although he had, in a general way, led an upright life, he was a wretched miser at heart. Christ, who knows what is in man, knew this. When this man, therefore, declared that he had kept all the commandments of God and desired to know what was yet lacking to complete his perfection, the Lord gives him a good lecture from which he can learn where his corruption is to be found, namely, in his infamous heart. Therefore the Lord tells him: "Sell that thou hast and give to the poor." But when the counselor hears this, he goes away sorrowful. Christ then adds: "A rich man shall hardly enter into the kingdom of heaven; It is easier for a camel to go through the eye of a needle, than for a rich man to enter into the kingdom of God." By these words, the disciples were so amazed that they exclaim: "Who then can be saved?" But what is Christ's answer? He adds: "The things which are impossible with men, are possible with God." In these words, Christ accordingly declares that with men, it is impossible to be rich and to be saved, but with God, all things are possible, and therefore this also. As soon as a man is converted to the Lord with his whole heart, he not only discards every vice and sin but also bids farewell to his wealth, saying to it without hypocrisy: "Thou art no longer my treasure; if therefore God again requires my money and goods of me. I will gladly give them back again; my heart is not attached to them. In a case like this, it is possible with God for a person to be very rich and yet to be saved. An especially beautiful example of this is that of Zaccheus. He had become very rich, partly by cheating others. As soon as he was converted to the Lord Jesus, he was prepared, if he had taken anything from any man by false accusation, to restore it to him fourfold and to give the half of his goods to the poor. If the communists' interpretation of the passage under consideration be correct, Christ would have said to Zaccheus: "The half is not enough; thou must sell all that thou hast and give to the poor." But of this, we read nothing. Christ, on the other hand, calls Zaccheus a true

Israelite, although he would give only half. Do not think that Zaccheus would not have been ready to give up all that he had, but he knew that God did not require it of him and that now, after his conversion, he could apply his possessions to a much better advantage than if he had been necessitated to give it all away at once., For if I give all I have to the poor, I can from that time forth extend no helping hand, nor would God require it of me.

Finally, the fourth passage adduced to prove that the principles of communism are biblical, is the parable of the laborers in the vineyard. The French communist Proudhon referred to the fact that, according to this parable, those who labored twelve hours received no more than those who labored nine, six, and three hours, yes, no more than those who labored but one hour. It is, however, strange that reference is made to this parable, for there is hardly any passage in the entire Bible more directly in conflict with communism. In the first place, we find here a householder who owns a vineyard. In the second place, we find laborers who were hired by the householder. In the third place, we notice here a contract for wages between the householder and his laborers, to which the householder afterwards refers. In the fourth place, we learn that these laborers were hired to labor twelve hours a day. In the fifth place, we learn that the master ascribes it all to his mercy and not to justice, that he gave the same wages to those who had labored only one hour as to those who had labored twelve. Every argument adduced in favor of communism on the basis of this parable thus falls to the ground.

These, then, are the Scripture passages adduced, in part

by believers, and in part by unbelievers, in defense of communism, which, however, either prove nothing or the directly opposite. From this, we may know that the efforts of the communists are opposed to Christianity. But we consider also that:

2. The efforts of the communists are in conflict with definite doctrines of Christianity.

We not only do not find anything in the Scriptures in defense of the communist system, but the Scriptures teach directly the opposite.

In the first place, it is in conflict with the scriptural doctrine of personal property, as contained in the seventh commandment. The seventh commandment teaches: "Thou shalt not steal," and with these words overthrows the entire system of communism. Do not misunderstand me. By this, I would by no means say that the communists desire to steal from others. No indeed, they say, on the contrary, that the rich are the thieves, as Proudhon has declared: "Holding possessions is theft." But this is what I would say: just as certain as the seventh commandment declares, "Thou shalt not steal," so certain it is that everyone should have his own personal property. For, if according to God's will, I should hold no personal property, God would not have forbidden others to take anything away from me. If no one is permitted to take anything from me, it is presupposed that I have something, and that, personal property. Consider this well.

The efforts of the socialists and communists are, in the

second place, opposed to the Scriptural doctrine of the Fifth commandment and other passages, according to which the government alone has the power of the sword. The communists do indeed preach from the housetops that they would have the new order of things, as suggested by them, introduced peaceably, but if they cannot accomplish it peaceably, they are ready to draw the sword and to fill the world with murder and conflagration, that by this means they may accomplish that upon which they claim the salvation of the world depends. But this conflicts with the Holy Scriptures, in which we have the word of God for these declare: "Thou shalt not kill," and respecting the government alone, they say, "he beareth not the sword in vain."

The efforts of the socialists and communists are, in the third place, contrary to the doctrine of the sanctity of the marriage state, as taught in the sixth commandment and elsewhere in the Scriptures. There are indeed many communists and socialists who do not sanction the community of wives, but they must acknowledge that there have been many communists who have taught this doctrine, e.g., Enfantin, Proudhon, Marx, and the so-called Egaliteurs. They were only the more consistent, and if the fearful catastrophe of communist rule should come upon us, those opposed to the abrogation of marriage could by no means hold the helm, but the equalization would be rigidly carried out, even to the extremity of introducing the community of wives.

These efforts are, in the fourth place, contrary to the differences between man and man as approved in the Scriptures. These differences pertain not only to parents and children, husband and wife, master and servant, but also to rich and poor. I need but refer to these doctrines, and every Christian must say: "Verily, if I will be a Bible Christian, I cannot possibly take part in these movements. The moment I connect myself with such an association, I must cast the Bible into the flames, or I am a wretched hypocrite who is carrying water on both shoulders and walks lame on both legs."

They are, in the fifth place, contrary to the doctrine of the Scriptures, that through all kinds of troubles, God would draw man to Himself, try him, and prepare him for Eternity. The communists (when I say "Communists," I refer to their leaders and not to everyone who, for want of experience, may have strayed into the organization) continually declare and preach it from the housetop, that they are sick of having the church hold out to them a prospective eternal life. They ridicule the idea that those who bear the cross with patience in this life can expect the glory of heaven in the life to come. "No," say they, "we would have our heaven here; in this life, we would be happy." Some say that it is, after all, very doubtful whether anything will be granted us in the future life; but others say; we are certain that all is a delusion: What Christian then could take part in the efforts of the communists and socialists?

They are, in the sixth place, opposed to the doctrine that man shall eat his bread in the sweat of his face. Those, therefore, who would make it appear that as soon as the communists have gained the supremacy, the golden times will come, that then all will be rich, inasmuch as all will then have access to the great treasury, these would have the people expect times of which there is no mention in the

Holy Scriptures. Every Christian is not only to eat his bread here on earth, that is, to have what he needs, but he shall eat it in the sweat of his face.

These efforts are, in the seventh place, contrary to the doctrine of the Scriptures that man shall not seek his happiness in this world, but in God and in the hope of a day of recompense and equalization, and in the hope of eternal life. These, therefore, who say that things shall no longer continue thus, that the human race shall, after all, finally become happy here below, speak against the Scriptures. God did not promise us happiness in this world. If we have food and raiment, we are to be therewith content. We must know that through many tribulations we enter into the kingdom of God. These are truths that the communists ridicule; however, those who firmly believe in Christ and His Word, are fully convinced that they are eternal and blessed truths. This is why we can have nothing to do with a system like that of the communists.

And finally, these efforts of the communists contradict the doctrine of the Scriptures, which says that sin is the source of all trouble in this world. For the Scriptures say: "Sin is a reproach to any people," and at another place: "Wherefore doth a living man complain, a man for the punishment of his sins?" (Lamentation 3:39.) The new communist movement is based upon this, that it is made to appear that all that is wanting in the world is a proper social organization. Should this once be effected, all trouble would be at an end. It is not so, however! The Scriptures tell us that God did indeed create man perfect in the beginning, but that man has fallen and that all trouble and wretchedness that exist in the world are but the consequence of this fall. Take sin out of the world, and you take all trouble and wretchedness out of the world. But as long as sin remains, there will be no heaven on earth. This would then be the second answer to the question which we are endeavoring to answer in these evening lectures.

FOURTH LECTURE

"Lord to whom shall we go? Thou hast the
words of eternal life? Thus Thy disciples
once answered Thy question: "Will Ye
also go away?" Thus, all, whoever became
Thy true disciples, had to exclaim, and
thus we too must exclaim. For to whom
else in all the world could we go for the
truth which we have found with Thee? To
whom in all the world could we go for
that grace which cancels our debt of sin
and which we have found with Thee?
And to whom in all the world could we
go for that blessed peace which we have
found with Thee?—
O grant then, that no mock wisdom or mock
comfort or feigned joy of this world may
occasion us ever to become unfaithful to
Thee.

*Open Thou also the spiritual eyes of those who
have as yet no knowledge of the salvation
to be found with Thee, that they may
know, that with Thee all things are to be
found for which the soul Of man longs,
that they too may come unto Thee and
remain with Thee unto death.
We will then praise and bless Thee for this
before Thy throne forevermore. Amen.*

———

There is one point yet which we must consider in our discussion of socialism and communism if we would proceed with fairness, justice, uprightness, and honesty. This is the accusation which socialism and communism make against the Christian religion and the Christian Church.

The first of these accusations is this: "The Church and the Christian religion are in league with capital," or to say the same thing in other words, "with the rich, the powerful, and consequently also with the oppressors, the tyrants."

"What else compares with the history of the Church," ask the communists, "than the history of the most atrocious wicked ness, of the plundering of the poor, and of bloody persecutions upon those who differed from them?"

And, my brethren, we cannot deny that in the name and under the covering of the Church and the Christian religion, some of the most heinous crimes have been committed, helpless people enslaved, impoverished and plundered, and streams of innocent bloodshed. Calling themselves the Christian Church, men have affirmed that, if necessary for the propagation of the Church, fire and the sword should be used. Calling themselves the Christian Church, they claimed that in defense of the Church, they had to burn the heretics. Calling themselves the Christian Church, they claimed a full right to demand of the lay members their bodily and earthly treasures brought to them by the Church. Calling themselves the Christian Church, they pretended that, for the salvation of the world, they had to gain the favor of the wealthy, had to gain riches, honor, respect, and power.

That all these abominations were committed by these who call themselves heads of the Christian Church and that these abominations were committed in league with princes, the great, the powerful, kings, and emperors is a fact which no one can deny. All these things are written on the pages of history in characters of blood, and no one can erase them.

It is not to be denied in this connection either, that even in the so-called Protestant State Church, many theologians united with the rich, the honored, the eminent, particularly with the princes, for the purpose of enslaving the common people to rob them as pertains to the body and soul, and to deprive them of all their rights.

But, brethren, what has this to do with the Christian religion and the Christian Church? The dark history of these abominations is not the history of the Christian Church, but rather the history of those TRAITORS AND ENEMIES OF THE CHURCH FOUND IN HER VERY BOSOM.

Or I ask you, when did Christ, or where do the Scriptures command such crimes?

Our Lord Jesus Christ was far from commanding His servants to propagate his kingdom by force with fire and sword, as did the lying prophet Mohammed; on the other hand, Christ strictly commanded His disciples: "Go and teach all nations and preach the gospel to every creature. He that believeth and is baptized shall be saved. but he that believeth not shall be damned." Observe then, that Christ did not give the secular sword into His disciples' hands; His Word is the weapon they were to use, and the means of propagating His kingdom was instruction and conviction; therefore, the Lord also told Peter, when he, in his carnal zeal, had drawn his sword in defense of his Lord; "Put up again thy sword into his place: for all they that take the sword, shall perish with the sword."

Our Lord Jesus was also far from requiring of his followers that they should persecute and kill the schismatic and the heretic, but to the contrary, He declares that the wheat and the tares shall remain together in the field until the time of harvest. And when those disciples desired that fire should fall from heaven because the Samaritans would not receive the Lord, the Lord declares unto them: "Ye know not what manner of spirit ye are of." He accordingly testifies: "It is not the spirit of the gospel to let fire fall from heaven upon the enemies of the Church."

Christ was also far from commanding His servants to conquer the kingdoms of this world for Him, and to seek after riches, honor, and power, but on the contrary, he publicly and solemnly declared in the presence of Pilate: "My kingdom is not of this world; if my kingdom were of this world, then would my servants fight, that I should not be delivered to the Jews: but now is my kingdom not from hence." Christ did not, as did the religious leaders of India and Egypt, intend to establish certain castes, as for example, the caste of the priesthood and the caste of the laymen: no, the New Testament knows of no privileged priesthood. Christ would have no difference made among the members of His Church. He plainly declares: "Ye know that the princes of the Gentiles exercise dominion over them, and they that are great exercise authority upon them. But it shall not be so among you, and whosoever will be chief among you, let him be your servant. One is your Master, even Christ; and all ye are brethren."

Christ did not by any means, either, advise his followers to slight and despise the poor as members of less importance than the rich; but to the contrary, Christ associated mostly with the poor and labored - mostly among them. He also says: "The poor have the gospel preached to them," and from among the poor He mostly gathered His Church. Therefore, the holy apostle Paul also says: "Brethren, God hath chosen not many noble after the flesh, but the weak things of the world."

Christ was also far from requiring His followers to associate particularly with the rich, commanding that they should do so because these had the greatest influence; that they should flatter them as those who had been especially preferred of God. There is, to the contrary, no book in all the world that speaks so contemptuously of the rich as the Book of Christ, i.e., the Holy Bible. In our last lecture, we already considered the significant words of the Lord: "It is easier for a camel to go through the eye of a needle than for a rich man to enter into the kingdom of God." In another place he says: "Blessed be ye poor; for yours is the kingdom of God." Again: "But woe unto you that are rich! for ye have received your consolation." And by St. Paul, the Holy Spirit warns all Christians: "They that will be rich, fall into temptation and a snare, and into many foolish and hurtful lusts, which drown men in destruction and perdition; for the love of money is the root of all evil, which while some coveted after they have erred from the faith, and pierced themselves through with many sorrows." James also says in the 5th chapter of his epistle: "Go to now, ye rich men, weep and howl for your miseries that shall come upon you. Your riches are corrupted, and your garments are moth-eaten. Your gold and silver is cankered, and the rust of them shall be a witness against you and shall eat your flesh as it were fire. Ye have heaped treasure together for the last days. Behold, the hire of the laborers who have reaped down your fields, which is of you kept back by fraud, crieth; and the cries of them which have reaped are entered into the ears of the Lord of Sabaoth. Ye have lived in pleasure on the earth, and been wanton; ye have nourished your hearts, as in a day of slaughter." And what is the apostles' admonition to the master as to his relation to the servant? He says: "Ye masters do the same things unto them, forbearing threatening, knowing that your Master also is in heaven; neither is there respect of persons with him." Is this flattering the rich? Is this requiring the Christians to associate with the rich, and that because they are rich?

And finally, my brethren, Christ or the Scriptures are far from warning the Christians against losing their respect for tyrants, lest they might fail to have the support of their strong arm; they, to the contrary, inform us that there has been no tyrant who did not come to a dreadful death through the terrible judgments of God. I need only refer you to Pharaoh, to Nebuchadnezzar, to Saul, to Manassa, to Herod. Yes, even more. When Solomon had been led away from the living God by his wives, his fall was also manifest in this, that he fearfully oppressed his people. He repented and died. The people then came to Solomon's successor, Rehoboam, and demanded of him that he should make the grievous burdens which were oppressing them, lighter. Rehoboam turned a deaf ear and, in his arrogance, sent the people away, —and what were the consequences according to the Scriptures? God, in his wrath, permitted it that ten tribes revolted, and thus five-sixths of the kingdom fell away from him.

You see from this, my brethren, that even if men, who are in league with the rich who oppress the poor, who are in league with the tyrants, call themselves Christians and are even found among their number, they are not Christians.

The first accusation of the socialists and communists against the Church and the Christian religion accordingly falls to the ground. For the Christian Church proper is not in league with oppression and tyranny, but is their enemy and a faithful friend of the poor and oppressed.

A second charge which the communists and socialists make against the Church and the Christian religion is this: The Christian Church has proved herself incapable of improving the miserable condition of the poor, incapable of removing the wrong relation which exists between the employer and the employed, and of bringing about such a state of affairs that all men might enjoy themselves in this world.

Brethren, it is even true that Christianity has, in reality, not destroyed the old system of oppression. Christianity has not only not destroyed the natural evil of the world, but the world has even continued in her wickedness since Christ came. But could such an effect be expected or required of any religion? Is it not the very object of religion to point out and to bring about the right relation between man and God and to reveal man's relation to a future life? The Church, by her religion, is to direct our attention to the proper relation which man is to sustain to man, and also to bring about such a relation. But the Church can do this only within her own bounds. Is not the use of physical power in direct conflict with the nature of the Church and the Christian religion? It is, therefore, a crying injustice to make religion responsible for failing to accomplish what she has no right and power to do.

To this must be added, that where the true Christian religion takes possession of the human heart, there it changes the relation between man and man and actually improves it. It is then that the relation between the rich and poor, between rulers and subjects, between employers and employees, and between the lofty and the low is really improved. That true faith produces these fruits when it takes possession of the heart, we learned in the last lecture. For when great necessity came upon the Christian congregation at Jerusalem, when the sword hung, as it were, by a hair over the Christian's head, the Christians had all things common, neither said any of them that aught of the things which he possessed was his own, and all only provided that none might be in want. And such will be men's relation to each other, where persons have become true Christians, who do not carry their faith at their tongue's end, but in whose hearts faith dwells.

Furthermore, everyone will admit that a final judgment of a matter can be given only after a trial. So then, let the socialists and communists give true Christianity a trial, i.e., let them become true Christians: what will be the consequence? They will acknowledge that Christianity is truly a divine, heavenly power for the conversion of man and for the changing of all the relations of men to each other; then they would see that if Christianity became universal, the sicknesses and weaknesses of this life, failures of crops, accidents, death, and other natural evils, would indeed not be put away; and they would see that it would put an end to the tyranny of tyrants and make of them just rulers, would take away the covetousness of the rich and make them liberal,[1] would take away the selfishness of the employers, so that they would look more to the common interests, and care more for the welfare of the laborer than for their own, would put an end to the envy of the poor and make them contented.

The socialists and communists will no doubt ridicule this; very few will believe it and will consequently remain in their misanthropy, i.e., enmity to mankind, and will, therefore, also continue to consider themselves in an unhappy condition. But, my brethren, we believe it. Why! we have experienced it and experience it daily, that Christianity has such power. It does not only make us blessed for the life to come, but it makes us blessed in this world, as it is written in the 128th Psalm: "Blessed is everyone that feareth the

Lord; that walketh in his ways. For thou shalt eat the labor of thine hands; happy shalt thou be, and it shall be well with thee." This we do not only read in the Scriptures, but we have also experienced it. Yes, we have also experienced what Asaph says in the 73rd Psalm: "Lord whom have I in heaven but thee? and there is none upon earth, that I desire besides thee. My flesh and my heart faileth, but God is the strength of my heart and my portion forever. But it is good for me to draw near to God; I have put my trust in the Lord God, that I may declare all thy works."

Let then every Christian take warning against the agitators of the socialists and communists. Their aim is a Fata Morgana, i.e., a brilliant, airy appearance, like a fairy castle. The pilgrim makes one more effort to reach this castle. He finally reaches the place where the bewitching atmospheric appearance was seen. And behold, it is gone, and the deceived wanderer is now surrounded with a darkness and trouble all the more dreary.

Oh then, my brethren, let us aim for some other object —that object which presents to us our heavenly calling in Christ Jesus. This is no Fata Morgana; this is reality, this is truth! There are indeed many who say: "No one has yet come from the other world to us to let us know that there is another life." But One has come from the other world to us, namely, Our Lord Jesus Christ, Who has sundered the bands of death and proclaimed to all of us: "I am the resurrection and the life; he that believeth in me, though he were dead, yet shall he live! And whosoever liveth and believeth in me, shall never die." Jesus be our guide then, and we will follow Him over mountains and through valleys, through prosperity and misfortune, through darkness and light!

Finally, the eternal and blessed light will make its appearance, then all our tears shall be wiped away, our sighings cease, and eternal unchangeable joy shall take possession of our hearts. Our Lord Jesus Christ, Who has obtained this for us, help that we may secure it. Amen.

Soli Deo Gloria

Appendix A

Johann the merry soap-boiler

by Friedrich von Hagedorn (1738)

> *A Steady and a skillful toiler,*
> *John got his bread as a soap-boiler,*
> *Earned all he wished, his heart was light,*
> *He worked and sang from morn till night.*
> *E'en during meals his notes were heard,*
> *And to his beer were oft preferred;*
> *At breakfast, and at supper, too,*
> *His throat had double work to do;*
> *He oftener sang than said his prayers,*
> *And dropped asleep while humming airs:*
> *Until his every next-door neighbor*
> *Had learned the tunes that cheered his labor,*
> *And every passer-by could tell*
> *Where merry John was wont to dwell.*
> *At reading he was rather slack,*

Studied at most the almanac,
To know when holidays were nigh,
And put his little savings by;
But sang the more on vacant days,
To waste the less his means and ways.

'Tis always well to live and learn.
The owner of the soap-concern —
A fat and wealthy burgomaster,
Who drank his hock, and smoked his
  k'naster,
At marketing was always apter
Than any prelate in the chapter,
And thought a pheasant in sour-krout
Superior to a turkey-poult;
But woke at times before daybreak
With heart-burn, gout, or liver-ache —
Oft heard our sky-lark of the garret
Sing to his slumber, but to mar it.

He sent for John, one day, and said:
"What's your year's income from your
  trade?"

"Master, I never thought of counting
To what my earnings are amounting
At the year's end: if every Monday
I've paid my meat and drink for Sunday,
And something in the box unspent
Remains for fuel, clothes and rent,
I've husbanded the needful scot,

And feel quite easy with my lot.
The maker of the almanac
Must, like your worship, know no lack,
Else a red-letter earnless day
Would oftener be struck away."

"John, you've been long a faithful fellow,
Though always merry, seldom mellow.
Take this rouleau of fifty dollars,
My purses glibly slip their collars;
But before breakfast let this singing
No longer in my ears be ringing:
When once your eyes and lips unclose,
I must forego my morning doze."

John blushes, bows, and stammers thanks,
And steals away on bended shanks,
Hiding and hugging his new treasure,
As it had been a stolen seizure.
At home he bolts his chamber-door,
Views, counts and weighs his tinkling store,
Nor trusts it to the savings-box
Till he has screwed on double locks.
His dog and he play tricks no more,
They're rival watchmen of the door.
Small wish has he to sing a word,
Lest thieves should climb his stair unheard.
At length he finds, the more he saves,
The more he frets, the more he craves;
That his old freedom was a blessing
Ill sold for all he's now possessing.

One day, he to his master went
And carried back his hoard unspent.

"Master," says he, "I've heard of old,
Unblest is he who watches gold.
Take back your present, and restore
The cheerfulness I knew before.
I'll take a room not quite so near,
Out of your worship's reach of ear,
Sing at my pleasure, laugh at sorrow,
Enjoy to-day, nor dread to-morrow,
Be still the steady, honest toiler,
The merry John, the old soap-boiler."

Notes

1. First Lecture

1. Translated by Rev. C. T. Steck
2. 2023 Publisher's note: Equalization of individuals, as understood today, is not a doctrine from Scripture. It is unclear what Walther is saying here, as he denies that God would be an equalizer on the next pages. Perhaps he is indicating something along the lines of Isaiah 40:4, where valleys are raised up, and mountains made low, or to Matthew 19:30 (Et al.) where Jesus speaks of the first being the last.
3. Naturam expellas furca, tamen usque recurret. (Horat, Ep. 1, 10, 24.)
4. 2023 Publisher's Note: The poem referred to here, which can be found at the end of this book, is likely *Johann the Merry Soap-boiler* by Friedrich von Hagedorn.

2. Second Lecture

1. See Luther's Works XVI, 157
2. See Erlangen Ed! of Luther's Works, Vol. 24, 260 also 262, and 283, 285.
3. See "Garantien der Harmonie und Freiheit. 1842," page 243 ff.
4. In English: "Guarantees of Harmony and Freedom"
5. Ibid., P. 229
6. Wernicke's History of World, V, 469.
7. 2023 Publisher's Note: Victor Considerant founded La Réunion, a 2,500 acre colony in Texas, in 1855, which hundreds of colonists joined. Considerant changed Fourier's ideas so that much of the structure of La Réunion was run along capitalist lines. Due to various factors, the colony collapsed in 1859.
8. Editor's Note to the 1947 edition: Walther's statements at the conclusion of this second lecture may be denied by some in the light of subsequent history. These people may say that Walther was wrong for Communism has been established in the Soviet Union since 1879. However, Walther is absolutely right. There is no actual communism in Russia today. Russia is as far from actual communism as any country could possibly be. The people of the Soviet Union are slaves in the hands of a few. Consequently Walther's statements still stand!

Honest communism carried out to the fullest meaning of the word, would result in dissatisfaction and chaos. Although true communism has never been attained even in the Soviet Union, that country nevertheless labors under a strict military dictatorship as ruthless as any the world has ever known!

9. 2023 Publisher's Note: the same may be said today. The primary remaining communist country, North Korea, is really nothing of the sort, but rather a strict and ruthless dictatorship.

3. Third Lecture

1. Communismus von W. Schulz in Bd. 2. der Supplemente zu Rotteck's und Welcker's Staatslexicon, Altona 1846. .S. 67.
2. 2023 Publisher's note: in so-called Communist states, art was not banished, but rather subverted to propagandistic purposes for the regime. Even so, these states were dictatorships and not true communes.

4. Fourth Lecture

1. 2023 Publisher's note: The term "liberal" here must be understood in the definition of the day. i.e,. in Webster's 1828 dictionary, the primary meaning is: 1. Of a free heart; free to give or bestow; not close or contracted; munificent; bountiful; generous; giving largely; ...

www.ingramcontent.com/pod-product-compliance
Lightning Source LLC
Chambersburg PA
CBHW060248030426
42335CB00014B/1624